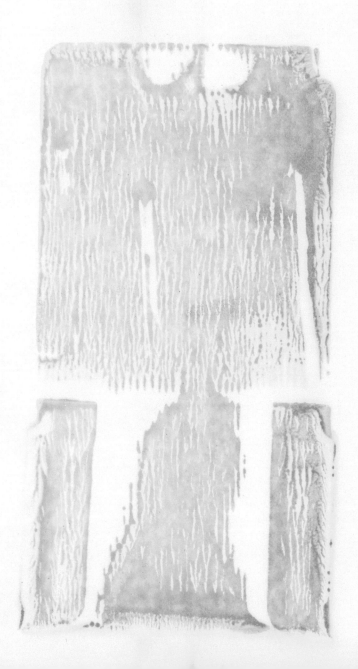

THE CRAFT OF P

PRENTICE-HALL
CONTEMPORARY COMPARATIVE POLITICS SERIES
JOSEPH LaPALOMBARA, Editor

W. PHILLIPS SHIVELY

University of Minnesota

Prentice-Hall, Inc.,
Englewood Cliffs, N. J.

THE CRAFT OF POLITICAL RESEARCH

A PRIMER

Library of Congress Cataloging in Publication Data

Shively, W   Phillips
     The craft of political research.

     (Prentice-Hall contemporary comparative politics
series)
     Bibliography: p.
     1. Political science—Methodology.   2. Political
science research.   I. Title.
JA73.S49   320'.01'8   73-13500
ISBN   0-13-188722-X
ISBN   0-13-188714-9 (pbk.)

THE CRAFT OF POLITICAL RESEARCH: A PRIMER
W. Phillips Shively

© 1974 by Prentice-Hall, Inc., Englewood Cliffs, New Jersey

Printed in the United States of America

10 9 8 7 6 5 4 3 2 1

PRENTICE-HALL INTERNATIONAL, INC., London
PRENTICE-HALL OF AUSTRALIA, PTY. LTD., Sydney
PRENTICE-HALL OF CANADA, LTD., Toronto
PRENTICE-HALL OF INDIA PRIVATE LIMITED, New Delhi
PRENTICE-HALL OF JAPAN, INC., Tokyo

to Barbara

CONTENTS

FOREWORD   xi

1   DOING RESEARCH   1

2   POLITICAL THEORIES AND RESEARCH TOPICS   12

3   THE IMPORTANCE OF DIMENSIONAL THINKING   30

4   PROBLEMS OF MEASUREMENT:
ACCURACY   45

5   PROBLEMS OF MEASUREMENT:
PRECISION   60

6   CAUSAL THINKING, AND THE DESIGN OF RESEARCH   79

7   INTRODUCTION TO STATISTICS:
MEASURING RELATIONSHIPS FOR INTERVAL DATA   102

8   INTRODUCTION TO STATISTICS:
FURTHER TOPICS ON MEASUREMENT OF RELATIONSHIPS   125

9   INTRODUCTION TO STATISTICS:
INFERENCE, OR HOW TO GAMBLE ON YOUR RESEARCH   144

10 WHERE DO THEORIES COME FROM?   163

SELECTED BIBLIOGRAPHY   168

INDEX   173

FOREWORD

The organization of the Contemporary Comparative Politics Series is based on a number of assumptions and guidelines that are worth calling to the reader's attention. Foremost among these is that the undergraduate student of comparative politics is less interested in political science than we might hope, but more capable of synthetic analysis than we may imagine. If this is so, then it would be an enormous mistake to pretend to organize an introductory series around one or more half-baked "theories" of politics or political systems—theories that are difficult for even the more hardened members of the profession to digest. It would seem equally debatable whether the undergraduate student has a strong desire to learn in depth the institutional arrangements and workings of any single political system, whether that system be as established as that of Great Britain or as new and exotic as that of Tanzania.

What, then, can we expect of those undergraduates who study comparative politics? First, I think that they are quickly turned off by simplistic or spurious efforts to lend the discipline a theoretical elegance it manifestly does not possess; second, that saturation treatments of single political systems are as unpalatable today when the countries are individually packaged as they were when several countries appeared between the same hard covers; third, that the undergraduates sitting in our classrooms might very well be turned on if they learned what sorts of things political scientists do and what kinds of knowledge of the political process they can glean from the things we do. These things, incidentally, would involve not merely data-gathering on some aspect of the political system, but also speculative and normative considerations about the relationship between politics and the good life. We can expect that if the things to be written and lectured about are carefully chosen and intelligently organized, the undergraduate will display a striking capacity to synthesize information and to develop skills in analyzing political phenomena at least as impressive as, say, those of a New York taxi driver, a voluble parent, or a political orator.

Another major assumption underlying the organization of the series is that the topics included should not reflect a commitment to an institutional or behavioral, normative or empirical approach. If members of the profession are still battling about such things, let them spare undergraduates the arid, scholastic, and essentially unproductive nature of such encounters. The authors of this series are neither bare-facts empiricists nor "cloud-ninety" political moralists; they neither sanctify nor abominate institutional or behavioral analysis, but would rather use whatever methods are available to enlighten the reader about important aspects of political life. To emphasize the important is also to be relevant, and our correlative assumption here is that the student who wants political science to be "relevant" does not mean by this that it should be banal, simple-minded, or unsystematic.

Since no series can tell us everything about politics, we have had to choose what we consider to be the important, relevant, and reasonably integrated topics. Such choices are always arbitrary to some extent. However, we have sought to accord attention to certain standards and ubiquitous institutions as well as to newer conceptual and analytical foci that have provoked a good deal of recent research and discussion. Thus, the series will have a volume on Comparative Legal Cultures, but another on Comparative Political Violence; it will include a fine volume on Constitutionalism and one on Revolutionary Movements.

This particular volume is intended to serve several needs. First, reading and comprehending it will greatly help the reader to understand and to evaluate other published materials in political science, including other volumes in this series. Second, *The Craft of Political Research* will introduce the reader to many of the things political scientists do as they gather, analyze, synthesize, and report about political phenomena.

Above all, Shively's beautifully crafted book will communicate the excitement and the joys of scientific research in the sometimes murky waters of politics. Everyone who meets the author even a small part of the way will be able to achieve greater precision of intellectual navigation.

Volumes to follow this one will represent what we believe is an interesting and useful mosaic that should be appealing to those who teach, those who learn about, and all of those who try to understand politics.

JOSEPH LAPALOMBARA

New Haven

THE CRAFT OF POLITICAL RESEARCH

DOING RESEARCH
1

To us who are engaged in doing it, scholarly research is an exciting, pleasurable activity. To some students, caught in the grind of daily and term assignments, this may not seem exactly the way to put it. But think of the people who can carry on research in a more relaxed way. It is a cliché that many professors would rather do research than teach, and I am pretty sure that research is so attractive to them not because of the usual reward system in universities—which admittedly weights it excessively—but because of the sheer fascination of doing it.

> *Francis' preoccupation with* DNA *quickly became full-time. The first afternoon following the discovery that A-T and G-C base pairs had similar shapes, he went back to his thesis measurements, but his effort was ineffectual. Constantly he would pop up from his chair, worriedly look at the cardboard models, fiddle with other combinations, and then, the period of momentary uncertainty over, look satisfied and tell me how important our work was. I enjoyed Francis' words, even though they lacked the casual sense of understatement known to be the correct way to behave in Cambridge. It seemed almost unbelievable that the* DNA *structure was solved, that the answer was incredibly exciting, and that our names would be associated with the double helix as Pauling's was with the alpha helix.*[1]

This is the way James D. Watson describes his and Francis Crick's search for the structure of the DNA molecule. *The Double Helix*, his account of their work, gives a good picture of the excitement of research. It is more gripping than most mystery novels.

Although research can be exciting in this way, the sad fact is that

[1] James D. Watson, *The Double Helix* (New York: Atheneum, 1968), p. 198.

writing papers for courses is too often nothing but a drag. First of all, course papers are tied to all sorts of rewards and punishments—your future earnings, the approval of others, and so on. All of the anxiety associated with these vulnerabilities comes, indirectly, to lodge on the paper. But this is probably the lesser cause for frustration in student research. After all, each of these anxieties also may be present for professional scholars. A more important reason for the student's lack of enthusiasm is the simple fact that his paper is generally regarded, by both teacher and student, as a practice run, going through the motions of scholarship. There usually is not enough time allowed for the student to think long and seriously about the subject, especially with other papers competing for his attention. And even when adequate time is allowed, there usually is a feeling on both sides that this is "just a student paper"—that it doesn't really matter how good it is, that a student will learn from doing the thing wrong. A student must have the chance to learn from his own mistakes, but this attitude toward his work cheats him of the pleasure and excitement which research can bring, of the feeling that he is creating something that no one ever saw before.

There is probably no way out of this dilemma. In a book such as this, I cannot give you the drama and excitement of original research. I can only give my own testimony, as one for whom research is very exciting. But I can introduce you to some selected problems you should be aware of if you want to do good research yourself or to evaluate the work of others. And I hope to make you aware of what a challenging game it can be, and of how important inventiveness, originality, and boldness are to good research.

SOCIAL RESEARCH

Social research is an attempt by social scientists to develop and sharpen theories which give us a handle on the universe. Reality, unrefined by theory, is too chaotic for us to absorb. Some people vote and others do not; in some elections there are major shifts, in others there are not; some bills are passed by Congress, others are not; economic development programs succeed in some countries, but fail in others; sometimes war comes, sometimes it does not. In order to have any hope of understanding why such things happen, in order to have any hope of controlling what happens, we must simplify our perceptions of reality.

Social scientists carry out this simplification by developing theories. A theory takes a set of similar things that happen—say, the development of party systems in democracies—and finds a common pattern in them, which allows us to treat all of these different occurrences as if they were simply repeated examples of the same thing. Instead of having to think about a large number of disparate happenings, we need to think of only a single pattern.

For example, in his book on political parties, Maurice Duverger was concerned with the question of why some countries develop two-party systems and others develop multi-party systems.[2] The initial reality was chaotic; scores of countries were involved, with varying numbers and types of parties present at different times in their histories. Duverger devised the theory that (1) if social conflicts overlap and (2) if the electoral system of the country does not penalize small parties, then the country will develop a multi-party system; otherwise, the country will develop a two-party system.

His idea was that where there is more than one sort of political conflict going on simultaneously in a country, and where the groups of people involved in these conflicts overlap, then there will be more than two distinct political positions in the country. (For example, a conflict between workers and the middle class might occur at the same time as a conflict between Catholics and non-Catholics. Then, if these groups overlapped so that some of the Catholics were workers and some were middle-class, while some of the non-Catholics were workers and some were middle-class, there would be four distinct political positions in the country—the Catholic worker position, the non-Catholic worker position, the Catholic middle-class position, and the non-Catholic middle-class position.) The appropriate number of parties would then tend to arise, with one party corresponding to each distinct position. However, Duverger thought that this tendency could be short-circuited if the electoral system were set up in such a way as to penalize small parties (for instance, by requiring that a candidate have a majority, rather than a plurality, of votes in a district). This would force some of the distinct groups to compromise their positions and merge into larger parties which would have a better chance of winning elections. Such a process of consolidation logically would culminate in a two-party system. To summarize the theory: a country will develop a two-party system (1.) if there are only two distinct political positions in the country, or (2) if in spite of the presence of more than two distinct political positions, the electoral law forces people of diverse positions to consolidate into two large political parties so as to gain an electoral advantage.

Having formulated this theory, Duverger no longer had to concern himself simultaneously with a great number of idiosyncratic party systems. He needed to think only about a single developmental process, of which all those party systems were examples.

Something is always lost when we simplify reality in this way. By restricting his attention to the number of parties competing in the system, for example, Duverger had to forget about many other potentially interesting things, such as whether any of the parties was revolutionary, or how many of the parties had any chance of getting a majority of the votes.

Note, too, that even in looking at the narrow topic that he had picked,

[2] Duverger, 1963, pp. 206–80.

Duverger chose deliberately to play down exceptions to his theory, despite the fact that these exceptions might have provided interesting additional information. Some party systems do not fit his theory as well as others. It might be that in one country, for which his theory predicted a two-party system, a multi-party system developed instead. Why was this so? Duverger might have cast around to find an explanation for the exception to his theory, and that explanation then could have been incorporated into the original theory to produce a larger theory. Instead, when faced with exceptions such as these, he chose to explain them away as accidents. It was necessary for him to do this in order to keep the theory simple and to the point. Otherwise, it might have grown as complex as the reality which it sought to simplify.

As you can see, there are costs in setting up a theory. Because the theory simplifies reality for us, it also generally requires that we both narrow the range of reality we look at and oversimplify even the portion of reality that falls within that narrowed range. As theorists, we always have to strike a balance between the simplicity of a theory and the number of exceptions we are willing to tolerate. We do not really have any choice. Without theories, we are faced with the unreadable chaos of reality.

Actually, what social scientists do in developing theories is not different from what everyone does in ordering reality and simplifying his perceptions of it. The social scientist just does the job in a more systematic and explicit way. Without theories, the student of society is trapped. He is reduced to merely observing events, without comment. Imagine a physicist—or a fruit-picker for that matter—operating in the absence of theory. All he could do if he saw an apple falling from a tree would be to duck, and he would not even know which way to move.

Social theory, then, is the body of all those theories developed by social scientists to explain human behavior. Political theory, which is what political scientists are concerned with, is part of social theory. It consists of all theories which have been developed to explain *political* behavior.

TYPES OF POLITICAL RESEARCH

There are different kinds of research in political science, deriving from the object for which you want to use the research and the particular stance you take toward the task of observing reality. This is important, because the way you conduct your research varies somewhat, according to which type of research it is.

There are two main ways in which one piece of research can be distinguished from another:

Table 1–1   Types of Political Research

	Applied	Recreational
Non-Empirical	Normative philosophy	"Formal" theory
Empirical	Engineering research	Theory-oriented research

1. Research may be directly intended to provide answers to particular problems. Or, it may be carried on more for its own sake, to add to our general understanding of politics. Thus, political research can be characterized by the *uses for which it is designed.*

2. Research also can vary in the stance it takes to the question of understanding reality. It may be intended primarily to discover new facts, or it may be intended to provide new ways of looking at old facts. Thus, political research can be characterized by the *extent to which it seeks to provide new factual information.*

These two dimensions roughly correspond to the old basic-applied and empirical-nonempirical distinctions. I have used them to form Table 1–1. Each of the major types of political research consists of a different combination of these two dimensions, as shown in the figure. "Normative philosophy" is applied and nonempirical; "engineering" research is applied and empirical; "formal theory" is recreational and nonempirical; and "theory-oriented" research is recreational and empirical.

"Normative philosophy" consists of argument about *what should be* in politics. Probably the oldest form of political research, it includes among its practitioners Plato, Karl Marx, Jerry Rubin, John Kenneth Galbraith, William F. Buckley, and others. It is applied research; that is, its goal is problem solving. This means that it is not intended so much to develop political theory as to use what political theory tells us about society and politics as a basis for making political decisions. It is also nonempirical in that it does not consist primarily of investigating matters of fact. It typically takes certain political facts as given and combines them with moral arguments to prescribe political action. A good example is John Stuart Mill's argument in "Considerations on Representative Government," in which he urges the adoption of democratic representative government because: (1) the chief end of government should be to facilitate the development in each citizen of his full potential (moral argument), and (2) democratic government, by giving the people responsibility, will do this (factual assumption).

Like normative philosophy, "engineering" research is geared to solving problems. But, unlike normative philosophy, it is empirical; it is concerned with ascertaining the facts needed to solve political problems. Some examples are: measuring the effects of various reapportionment methods, trying to design a diplomatic strategy which would bring about disarmament, and designing methods of riot control.

At present the two applied forms of research have only weak support in academic political science. Political engineering is rarely taught at all. Normative philosophy is taught extensively, and research is carried on under that name, but generally this means the *history* of normative philosophy and its development, not the active forming of normative arguments. For both forms of applied research, we must look mainly outside academic life to such sources as the RAND Corporation and the *New York Review of Books*.

It is hard to say exactly why this is so. It might be ascribed to a desire to avoid partisanship, except that the same tendency can be observed in other fields which deal in less political questions—the natural sciences, for example, in which "engineering" is carefully kept outside the regular departments and is often relegated to a separate school. It is not that applied research is unstimulating, as anyone who has worked through Marx's dialectic or some of the more complex formulas for the reapportionment of legislatures must realize.

I have labeled the other side of "applied" research "recreational." It is usually called "pure" or "basic" research, but this carries the unpleasant implication that applied research is either impure or ephemeral. The choice of the term "recreational" to describe this type of research is really not as flippant as it might seem, for this is research which is carried on for its own sake, in order to improve political theory. It is carried on for the twin pleasures of exercising our minds and increasing our understanding of things. In a high sense of the word, it is "recreation."

"Formal" theory, largely a post-World War II phenomenon, is the most recently introduced form of political research. Like normative philosophers, formal theorists posit certain facts about politics. Their concern is to take these posited facts, or assumptions, and derive theories from them. Their end goal is to develop reasonably broad and general theories based on a small number of agreed-upon assumptions. In order to accomplish this, they work with precise, usually mathematical, statements of their assumptions.

A good example of formal theory—in fact, a work by which many would date the emergence of formal theory as a distinct field in political science—is Anthony Downs' *An Economic Theory of Democracy*.[3] Downs builds a wide-ranging theory from a set of assumptions which include, for example: (1) voters and parties behave rationally; (2) political conflict occurs on only one issue at a time; and (3) political events are not perfectly predictable. Some of the predictions generated from his theory are: (1) in

[3] Downs, 1957.

a two-party system, parties will tend to agree very closely on issues; in a multi-party system, they will not; (2) it may be rational for the voter to remain uninformed; and (3) democratic governments tend to redistribute income. (The reader is asked to realize that a brief sampling, such as this does even more than the usual violence to a rich net of theories.) It is important to emphasize that this sort of work is almost solely an exercise in deduction. All of the conclusions derive directly from a limited set of explicit assumptions. Downs' purpose in this is simply to see where the assumptions he started with lead him. Presumably, if the assumptions produced an unreasonable result, he would go back and reexamine the assumptions.

Like normative philosophy, formal theory interacts with empirical research. Formal theorists usually try to start with assumptions which are in accord with existing knowledge about politics, and at the end they may compare their final models with the existing knowledge. But they are not themselves concerned with turning up new factual information.

Most research and teaching in political science is of the fourth type suggested in Table 1–1—"theory-oriented" research. This type of research is concerned with expanding our knowledge of what happens in politics and of why it happens as it does. Like political engineering, it is empirical; it is concerned with discovering facts about politics. But unlike engineering, which deals with facts only for their usefulness in specific political problems, this research deals with them in order to develop new political theories or to change or confirm old ones. Accordingly, the most important activity in this research is the development of theories linking observed facts about politics. In engineering, facts are sought out if they are needed to solve a problem; here they are sought out if they will be useful in developing theories.

Duverger's work, which has been described already, is an example of "theory-oriented" research. Another good example is a test by Eric Nordlinger of the theory that military governments in the developing nations tend to encourage economic modernization.[4] Nordlinger measured the amount of influence that the military have in the governments of seventy-four countries, and also measured various aspects of economic modernization in these countries. He concluded that a powerful military tends to *retard* economic modernization. He further developed an explanation of why this should be so, and brought in other variables, such as the size of the middle class, to predict exceptions to his theory.

THE RESEARCH "MIX"

Practically no research is a *pure* example of any of the types I have presented here. These are abstract distinctions, types of emphasis found in particular

[4] Nordlinger, 1970.

pieces of research. Generally, any specific piece of work is a mix of more than one of the types. One or another usually will be emphasized, but generally there will be some interaction between different types of research in any person's work. Two examples may help illustrate this point.

First, let us look a bit more closely at normative philosophy, using Karl Marx's work as an example. Marx's theory of the dialectic is primarily a work in normative philosophy. His argument takes the form: "Because _____ aspects of the human condition today are bad, and because the state and the economy function in _____ ways to produce these bad effects, we should strive to change the state and the economy in _____ ways, which will eliminate the bad effects." But Marx was less willing than Mill was, in the argument to which we have referred already, simply to *assume* the factual portions of his argument. Instead, he spent years of research trying to work out the precise economic effects of capitalism. Anyone developing normative theories about politics must include some sort of facts about politics in his theory. He may be relatively more willing to assume these facts out of his general experience and from the research of others, as Mill was, but on the other hand he may wish, like Marx, to investigate the factual basis of his theory himself.

It is characteristic of normative philosophy, though, that the researcher need not feel that he is *required* to produce the full factual basis for his argument. Normative philosophy differs in this respect from the empirical types of political research.

The distinction is an important one. For one thing, the fact that the normative philosopher is not required to provide evidence for all his assumptions leaves him free to devote more energy to other parts of his task. But more importantly, he often needs to assume facts which cannot possibly be tested against reality. The normative philosopher must be free to imagine realities which have never existed before, and these, of course, cannot be "tested." If the normative philosopher were held to the same standards of factual evidence as his empirical counterparts, all utopian dreams would have to be thrown out.

As a second example of the way in which types of research are mixed in any one work, let us look at a case in which researchers working on a primarily "engineering" project were forced to develop a theory in order to make sense out of their work. A group of sociologists, led by Samuel Stouffer, studied the morale of American soldiers during World War II for the Army.[5] Stouffer and his coworkers were puzzled by the fact that very often a soldier's morale had little to do with his objective situation.

For instance, MPs were objectively less likely to be promoted than were members of the Army Air Corps. Of Stouffer's sample of MPs, 24 percent were noncommissioned officers, compared with 47 percent of the Air

[5] Stouffer *et al.*, 1949.

Corpsmen. Paradoxically, however, the MPs were much more likely than the Air Corpsmen to think that soldiers with ability had a good chance to advance in the Army. This sort of paradox occurred a number of times in their study, and the researchers felt they had to make some sense of it if their research was to help the Army improve morale.

They did this by developing the theory of relative deprivation to account for their odd findings. According to this theory, a person's satisfaction with his condition is not a function of how well-off he is objectively, but of whether his condition compares favorably or unfavorably with a standard that he perceives as normal.

The fact that so many men in the Air Corps were NCOs apparently made men there feel that promotion was the normal thing. Those who were not promoted were disappointed, and those who were promoted did not feel particularly honored. Among the MPs, on the other hand, promotion was sufficiently infrequent that *not* being promoted was seen as the norm. Those who were not promoted were not disappointed, and those who were promoted felt honored. Thus, paradoxically, the Air Corpsmen, who were more likely to be promoted, felt that chances for promotion in the Army were poor, and the MPs, who were less likely to be promoted, felt that chances for promotion in the Army were good!

I have mentioned these two examples to illustrate my point that most research work involves some mix of the types of research which I originally set out. Indeed, a mix is so much the usual situation that when I tried to make a rough head count of the frequency of the different types of research in political science journals, I was unable to do so. I found that I was unwilling to assign most articles simply to one or another of the categories. It is just not the case that a researcher is a "normative philosopher," an "engineer," a "formal theorist," or a "theory-oriented empirical researcher." These types interact in the work of every political scientist.

The fact that most research involves a mix of the types does not mean that the distinctions are unimportant, however. Generally, one type of research is dominant in any given piece of work. The type of research involved, as we shall see, has a lot to do with the way a study should be set up and the standards by which it is judged.

EVALUATING DIFFERENT TYPES OF RESEARCH

It is dangerous to set down simple standards for good research. Research, like any creative work, should be evaluated subjectively, with informal and rather flexible criteria. But I will risk suggesting two standards for research which will serve as examples of the way in which the type (or types) of research we are doing dictates the way we should conduct that research.

In the first place, in either form of empirical research, the researcher should be held responsible for *demonstrating the factual basis of his conclusions*. In either form of nonempirical research, this is not necessary, though a normative argument may be made more convincing, or an exercise in formal theory may be made more interesting, by providing evidence for the factual basis on which its assumptions rest.

In the second place, good research of any sort should be *directed to an interesting problem*. But what sort of problem is "interesting" depends largely on the motivation of the study. For either sort of applied research, problems should be chosen which are of real importance for contemporary policy. Today an argument about civil disobedience, for example, makes a more interesting problem in normative theory than an argument about the problem of dynastic succession; a few hundred years ago the reverse may have been the case. In other words, applied research should be "relevant," in the common usage of the word.

Recreational research, on the other hand, requires problems which will have a substantial impact on existing bodies of theory. Many topics which are of considerable importance to an engineer show little promise for theory-oriented research. Similarly, many promising topics for recreational research are not directly "relevant."

For example, research on the difference between men's and women's voting in Iceland in the 1920s and 1930s sounds absurd from the standpoint of an engineer. But these voting patterns, occurring just after the extension of the vote to women, might be important for theories of how voting patterns become established among new voters.

How to choose an interesting problem is one of the most difficult and challenging parts of empirical research. I shall discuss this in some detail in Chapter 2.

In general, this book is concerned with empirical research. For instruction in formal theory and normative theory, which involve logical deduction and moral argument, one really should look to philosophy, mathematics, and rhetoric. Within empirical research, I shall devote somewhat more attention to theory-oriented research than to engineering. There are two reasons for this: (1) it is the more common kind of research in political science; and (2) it poses rather more difficult instructional problems than engineering does.

POLITICAL THEORIES AND RESEARCH TOPICS

2

In this chapter we shall look more closely at the nature of political theories and at the factors that enter into deciding to do research on a particular theory. Along the way I shall discuss some standards to use in deciding whether a theory is weak or strong.

Although this chapter deals with political theories, you should not assume that it is important only for what I have called "theory-oriented" research. In fact, the object of "engineering" research may also be a political theory of some sort. Many engineering problems can be solved only by developing a theory to explain why the phenomenon you want to control occurs, so that you can control it by making adjustments in the factors that cause it. Much applied research on the problem of enriching the education of underprivileged children, for example, has had to concern itself with developing theories to explain why one child learns things more quickly than another. The Stouffer study, cited in Chapter 1, is another example of an engineering study in which it was necessary to develop a theory. In that case, Stouffer and his collaborators had to explain why some soldiers had higher morale than other soldiers. This was necessary if they were to think up ways to raise morale in the Army as a whole.

On the other hand, many engineering studies do not require that a theory be developed; they simply involve measuring things which need to be measured. Taking the United States census is one example of such engineering research. The Gallup Poll, studies measuring the malapportionment of state legislatures, studies measuring the relative military strength of various countries, and so on, are additional examples.

In sum, engineering research may or may not involve the development of political theories; theory-oriented research always does. Theory is a tool in the one type of research; it is an end in itself in the other. Thus, regardless of which type of research you are concerned with, it is worth taking a closer look at the nature of theory.

In the social sciences, theories generally are stated in a causal mode: "If X happens, then Y will follow as a result." The examples which we looked at in Chapter 1 were all of this form. In the Duverger example, *if* a certain configuration of political conflicts existed, and *if* the country adopted a certain electoral law, *then* the number of political parties in the country would tend to grow or shrink to a certain number. In Nordlinger's study, *if* the military take over a government, and *if* the middle class is of a given size, *then* the country's economic development can be expected to decline.

A causal theory always includes some phenomenon which is to be explained or accounted for. This is the *dependent variable*. In Duverger's theory, the dependent variable was the number of parties. A causal theory also includes one or more factors which are thought to affect the dependent variable. These are called the *independent variables*. Duverger used two independent variables in his theory: the nature of social conflicts in a country and the country's electoral system.

All of these are called "variables" simply because it is the variation of each which makes it of interest to us. If party systems had not varied—that is, if each country had had exactly the same number of parties—there would have been nothing for Duverger to explain. And if one or the other of his independent variables had not varied, that factor would have been useless to him in explaining the dependent variable. For instance, if all countries had had the same electoral system, then the variations in party systems which puzzled him could not have been due to differences in the countries' electoral systems, inasmuch as there were none.

The dependent variable is called "dependent" because, *in terms of the particular theory used,* it is thought to be the result of some other factors (the independent variables). What it looks like "depends" on what those other factors look like. Similarly, the independent variables are called "independent" because, *in terms of the particular theory,* they are not taken as determined by anything in particular.

The same variable may be an independent variable in one theory and a dependent variable in another. For instance, one theory might use the social status of an individual's father as an independent variable to explain the individual's social status, which is taken as the dependent variable. Another theory might use an individual's social status as an independent variable to explain something else, perhaps the way he votes.

WHAT DOES GOOD THEORY LOOK LIKE?

Three things are important if we are to develop good, effective theories:

1. *Simplicity.* A theory should give us as *simple* a handle on the universe as possible. It should use no more than a few independent variables. It would not be very useful to develop a theory which used thirty variables, in intricate combinations, to explain why people vote the way they do. Such a theory would be about as chaotic and as difficult to absorb as the reality it sought to simplify.

2. *Predictive accuracy.* A theory should make *accurate predictions.* It does not help to have a simple, broad theory which gives predictions that are not much better than one could get by guessing.

3. *Importance.* A theory should be *important.* What makes a theory important is different in engineering research than in theory-oriented research, so we shall consider them separately:

In engineering research, a theory should address a problem which really is pressing. This is a subjective judgment, of course, but as a check on yourself you should try to justify choosing to do research on this particular problem. You need to justify this not only to yourself but also to your audience. Your research report should include some discussion of the importance of the problem and of possible applications for your findings. It may seem unnecessary for me to point this out, but it is an important part of the engineering research project, and it is often carried out sloppily and in an incomplete way. Students have been known, for example, to simply turn in a computer printout as a paper, because "the results are obvious." True, the *obvious* results may be obvious, but an imaginative researcher who sits down and thinks about it for a while may be able to point up additional, more varied ways in which his findings can be used.

In theory-oriented research, the theory should give a handle on as big a portion of the universe as possible; that is, it should apply broadly and generally. It is easy to develop a trivial theory. A theory of the organization of borough presidencies in New York City, for example, might predict quite accurately for that specific question. But, inasmuch as the borough presidents have little power, it would not help us very much in reducing the chaos of even New York politics, let alone the chaos of politics in general.

When we say that a theory should apply "broadly" and "generally," we are referring not only to how varied a selection of items from reality the theory deals with, but also to how great a variety of preexisting theories are affected by the new theory. A theory can attain great generality rather economically if it helps to recast older theories, each of which involves its own portion of reality. Thus, a theory of electoral change might take on importance partly from the phenomena it explained directly—changes in people's votes—but it would be much more important if it could be shown to have significant implications for other areas of social theory—democratic theory, general theories of attitude change, or whatever. In effect, it would perform two simplifying functions. It would serve to simplify the portion of reality which it sought to explain directly. And it would serve to simplify those portions of reality dealt with *by all the other theories* as well.

In the example above, a theory to explain the organization of borough presidencies in New York, the theory accrues so little importance directly as to look absurd. But it might be possible, if the borough presidents were taken as examples of some broader concept in urban politics, for the study to borrow importance from the broader theories it affected. The borough presidencies might, for example, serve as a useful microcosm for studying the workings of patronage.

If a theory can suceed reasonably well at meeting these three criteria —importance, simplicity, and predictive accuracy—then it will be useful as a tool for simplifying reality. Such a theory is sometimes described as "elegant."[1] One difficulty in creating elegant theory is that trying to meet any one of the three basic criteria listed here tends to make it harder for you to meet the other two. In the example of Duverger's theory, we saw that he might have improved the accuracy of his theory's predictions by bringing in additional explanatory variables; but this would have reduced the simplicity of the theory. Similarly, an attempt to make a theory more general often will cost us something in either the simplicity of the theory or the accuracy of its predictions.

It appears to be particularly hard to achieve elegant theory in the social sciences, compared with other scientific areas. Man's behavior is more complex than the behavior of physical objects. It may even be that his behavior is largely beyond explanation. On the other hand, it may be that his behavior can be understood, but that we have not yet come up with the first good social theory which could show the potential of our field. At any rate, it is rare for theory in the social sciences to achieve elegance. If a theory's predictions are reasonably accurate, it is usually because the scope of the theory is restricted or because many of the exceptions to the theory have been absorbed into it as additional variables, making it very complex.[2]

The fact that most social science theory is not very elegant does not mean that it is not good. The real test of a theory's value is whether its subject matter is important and how close it has come to elegance, *given*

[1] The choice of this word typifies the esthetic pleasure—and the vanity—with which researchers approach their work.

[2] Another reason for the difficulty of attaining elegance in social research, of course, is simply that most social science terms are imprecise and ambiguous. This is a problem which I shall address in Chapter 3.

Table 2–1   Percent Having Some Sort of Party Identification

	France	USA
Know Father's Party	79.4	81.6
Do Not Know Father's Party	47.7	50.7

that subject matter. If it is important to understand man's behavior, then it is important to try to develop theories about it, even if things do not fall as neatly into place as we would like.

AN EXAMPLE OF "ELEGANT" RESEARCH: PHILIP CONVERSE

In his article "Of Time and Partisan Stability," Philip Converse comes about as close to developing an "elegant" theory as one can commonly do in the social sciences.[3] His study is worth looking at in some detail.

Converse takes as his dependent variable the strength of the "party identification" of individuals—their sense that they are supporters of one or another of the political parties. In an earlier study, he and Georges Dupeux had found that, whereas about 75 percent of Americans who were polled identified with some political party, a similar poll conducted in France showed that less than 45 percent of the respondents did so.[4] Other studies had shown high levels of party identification in Britain and Norway, and lower levels of party identification in Germany and Italy. Because the overall extent to which citizens of a particular country felt bound to the existing parties seemed likely to have something to do with how stable politics in that country would be, Converse wanted to know why the level of party identification varied as it did from country to country.

At the time of their French study, he and Dupeux had found that the difference between France and the United States seemed to be explained almost wholly by the fact that more Americans than French had some idea of what party their fathers had identified with. As we can see in Table 2–1, within each row there was practically no difference between the French and American levels of party identification.

In both countries about 50 percent of those who did not know their fathers' party expressed identification with some party themselves. About 80

[3] Converse, 1969.

[4] Converse and Dupeux, 1962.

percent of those who did know their fathers' party did so. Thus, the difference between the two countries was apparently a result of the fact that the Americans knew their fathers' party so much more frequently than the French did.

At the time, Converse and Dupeux accepted this as an interesting fact and did not elaborate on it. But in "Of Time and Partisan Stability," Converse uses the earlier finding to suggest a general theory of the process by which countries developed stable patterns of party preference.

In doing so he brings two strands of theory together. First, he reasons that the difference between France and the United States could be explained easily if the previous generation in France had, in fact, included very few voters who identified with a party. It could have been, of course, that the difference was due to the fact that the French did not talk to their children about politics as much as the Americans did. But for the purposes of argument, Converse chose to assume that this was not the case. He then shows that if his assumption about the previous generation's low level of party identification were true, one could expect the next generation in France to be much more like the Americans. Also, if the assumption were true, France must be moving toward the level of party identification found in the United States, Britain, and Norway. (This is explained in the box, "Markov Chains.")

Converse further reasons that the 80 percent and 50 percent figures might be universally true. (He only *knows* that they hold for France and the United States.) If this is so, then France and the United States might both simply be examples of a general process which all countries undergo when their citizens are first given the vote. In the first election, none of the voters in the country identify with a party. But 50 percent of that generation's children would identify with a party; and gradually, the country's voters would reach a stable level of party identification (see box). According to this scheme, the relatively low level of party identification in France must have resulted because the vote was extended later and less completely there than in America. (French women, for one thing, were first given the vote in 1945.) Thus, France must be at an earlier stage of the process than America.

The second strand of theory comes into play when Converse ties his theory of national development to some older findings on individual voters in the American electorate. Voting studies commonly have shown that within an individual's life span, the older he is the more likely he is to identify strongly with a party. Moreover, this has been shown to be a result of how long he has been exposed to the party by being able to vote for it, rather than of his age itself.[5]

Working from these two angles, Converse develops a simple theory which predicts the strength of a voter's party identification from just two

[5] This was first demonstrated in Campbell *et al.*, 1960, pp. 161–64.

Markov Chains

Converse's reasoning is based on some cute, simple mathematics which you can play with for yourself. If the rates of transferring identifications are in fact the same in two countries, then even though the countries differ greatly in the level of identification at present, we would expect them to converge rapidly. For example, Converse and Dupeux estimated for France and the United States that about 80 percent of those whose fathers had identified with a party developed an identification of their own, and that, of those whose fathers had not identified with a party, about 50 percent developed an identification of their own. Given these figures, and assuming that party identifiers have the same number of children as nonidentifiers, then if 30 percent of the population of country A presently identify with a party, and 90 percent of the population of country B presently identify with a party, in the next generation we would expect to see

$$(0.8 \times 30\%) + (0.5 \times 70\%) = 59\%$$

of country A having an identification, and

$$(0.8 \times 90\%) + (0.5 \times 10\%) = 77\%$$

of country B having an identification. In the next generation after that, we would expect to see

$$(0.8 \times 59\%) + (0.5 \times 41\%) = 67.7\%$$

of country A having an identification, and

$$(0.8 \times 77\%) + (0.5 \times 23\%) = 73.1\%$$

of country B having an identification. Thus, in two generations the two countries, which had started out being quite different, would have moved to similar levels of party identification. The process involved here, called a "Markov chain," is described in J. Kemeny, J. Snell, and G. Thompson, *Introduction to Finite Mathematics* (Englewood Cliffs, N.J.: Prentice-Hall, Inc., 1957), pp. 171–78.

things: (1) the number of years he has been eligible to vote (which is partly a matter of how old he is, and partly a matter of how long elections have been held in his country); and (2) the likelihood that his father had identified with a party (which is taken as a function of the portion of the father's adult life that elections in which he was eligible to vote were held in the country). The first of these derives from the older studies of individual development, the second from his theory based on France and the United States. Thus, essentially, strength of party identification is predicted from the individual's age and the length of time that his country has been holding elections.

A few examples of predictions from his theory are: (1) at the time elections are first held in a country, the pattern which we typically see in Europe and America (the young being weakly identified, the old strongly) would not hold; all would identify at the same low levels; (2) if elections were interrupted in a country (as in Germany from 1933 to 1945), levels of party identification should decline at a predictable rate; (3) *if* the transition rates for all countries were roughly the same as for France and the United States, then all electoral democracies should converge over the next couple of generations toward a single level of party identification, with about 72 percent identifying with a party.

Thus, although Converse's theory is quite simple, it is applicable to a very wide variety of questions. It simultaneously explains individual behavior and characteristics of political systems. It implies a more or less universal form of political development at the mass level—with a prediction of initial, but rapidly decreasing, potential for electoral instability in a new electorate. And it includes the startling suggestion of a convergence of "mature" electorates to a common level of party identification approximately equal to that of Britain, Norway, or the United States.

The theory is simple, and it is broadly applicable. What is more, it seems to predict fairly accurately, thus fulfilling the third criterion for "elegance." Using data from Britain, Germany, Italy, the United States, and Mexico to test the theory, Converse found that the theory predicted quite well for all five countries.

TO QUANTIFY OR NOT?

A side issue in the question of how to develop elegant theory is the old chestnut: "Should political science be 'quantitative' or not?" There has been much rhetoric spilled over this. As long ago as 1956, James Prothro called the dispute "the nonsense fight over scientific method," but it has not cooled noticeably in the intervening years.[6]

It is a bit hard to pin down exactly what the term "quantitative" means, but generally research which pays a good deal of attention to *numerical* measures of things, and tends to make *mathematical* statements about them, is considered "quantitative." Research which is less concerned with measuring things numerically, and which tends to make *verbal* statements about them, is considered relatively less "quantitative."

---

[6] Prothro, 1956.

Anything in political science can be stated with varying degrees of quantification. To give a crude example: "The average length of Congressmen's service in the House increased from 1880 to 1965 by an average of .78 years every decade; the rate of increase was .68 years per decade before 1922, and .86 years per decade after 1922," says approximately the same thing as "From 1880 to 1965, Congressmen steadily increased the length of time they served in the House; the change proceeded a bit more rapidly in the latter half of that period." The first form of the statement gives more precise information, but the sense of the two statements is the same.

Each approach involves costs and benefits for research. Most people would agree that precise information is more useful than imprecise information, all other things being equal. But it may be that the time and attention spent in gathering precise data make it difficult for the researcher to see wider aspects of a theory. Also, because some kinds of data by their very nature can be gathered in a more precise form than can other kinds, there is a danger that attention to precision in our data may restrict our attention to those variables we can measure more precisely. It is striking, for instance, how little the Presidency is studied by political scientists. This may well be due to the difficulty of getting "hard" data on what goes on in that office.

I shall develop this question further in Chapter 5. For our purposes here, the important thing is to see what relationship degrees of quantification bear to elegance in research.

First of all, the particular subject we are studying affects the extent to which it is possible for us to quantify. In election studies, there is considerable scope for quantification. Election records from earlier elections usually are kept in fairly good shape; the results of many attitude studies are available; and most voters do not regard their actions as something about which they need to maintain secrecy. Thus, the quantitative researcher is able to do a great deal. In Soviet studies, or in studies dealing with the United States Presidency, on the other hand, sources of quantitative data are quite restricted, and most research must be relatively nonquantitative.

In each of these fields, however, and certainly in the rest of political research, work is possible in either a primarily quantitative or primarily nonquantitative mode. In fact, it is probably best that research with varying degrees of quantification be carried on in any given field of political research, for the different levels of quantification complement each other. Typically, less quantitative research provides greater breadth, greater openness to totally new theories, and a greater awareness of the complexity of social phenomena. More quantitative research, on the other hand, is more likely to produce simple, usable theories; and it is certainly more likely to give us a clear idea of how accurate a theory's predictions are. Thus, certain aspects of elegance can be more easily attained through one kind of research, others through the other kind. But no particular degree of quantification has a corner on elegance.

CHOOSING A TOPIC

The choice of a topic for research is intimately bound up with the elegance of what comes out of the research. In choosing a topic, of course, the first thing to do is to choose a general area that is interesting and significant for you. By choosing to study political science you already have begun to narrow the field, and you certainly will narrow things more than that before you are ready to begin. There is no difficulty in this; you just follow your interests.

But once you have chosen a general area to work in, picking a particular topic to research is difficult. This is the one most critical step in doing research. It is also the most difficult aspect of research to teach anyone. It is at this step—seeing that a problem exists and that there is a good chance that you can find an interesting answer to it—that originality and talent are most critical.

The important thing in choosing a topic is to pick one which is likely to give you new and elegant results. This implies two things: (1) you want to choose a topic from which you expect to get new results—that is, you want a topic whose results are likely to alter existing opinion on a subject; and (2) you want your results, as much as possible, to attain the three criteria for elegance: simplicity, predictive accuracy, and importance.

ENGINEERING RESEARCH

Choosing a topic is somewhat simpler in engineering research than it is in theory-oriented research. Here, it is primarily a question of using your time and talents efficiently. The topic should be one on which you think elegant research is possible. That is, it should be one which deals with a pressing problem, and one on which you think you are likely to come up with findings which are accurate and which are simple enough to be useful. At the same time, it should be one for which your results will be new. You will want to pick a problem in which you will either not duplicate a previous study or duplicate a previous study which you think produced mistaken results. There is no sense in wasting your time running over ground that has already been worked, unless you think you are likely to correct earlier work.

One difficulty in choosing the topic is that you probably will have to compromise among the goals. You may decide that for the problem that is nearest your heart, there simply is not enough material available to let you study it satisfactorily. Many topics relating to defense or to the executive are of this sort. Or it may be that a topic interests you, not because it deals with the most pressing problem you can think of, but because you have seen some research on it that you think would be rather easy to correct.

The main thing to do in looking for a topic is to read. You should read so that you are certain you are picking an important problem, and you should read to find out how likely it is that your topic will yield useful results. Finally, you should read to see what other work has been done on the problem, or on similar problems, so that you will see where you are most likely to produce results that are new.

THEORY-ORIENTED RESEARCH

It is not easy to choose a topic in engineering research, but choosing a topic in theory-oriented research is still harder. Deciding what topic is likely to produce important results is much more difficult in the latter than in the former.

You will recall that if theory-oriented research is to be important, it should have a broad and general effect on theory. This effect can be achieved either directly, through the phenomena it explains, or indirectly through the variety of other theories it affects. Similarly, to be "new," the research results must either produce totally new theories or lead to some change in the status of older theories.

This means that in framing any topic for research, you are involved at once in the full body of political science theory, for a single piece of research may simultaneously affect many different theories. Research on how a Congressional committee reaches its decisions, for example, can affect theories about power in Congress, general theories about committees and organizations, theories about executive-Congressional relations, theories about elite political behavior, and so on.

In particular, the task of deciding which research topic is going to produce the greatest change in the status of existing theories is very difficult. This requires not only that you be familiar with as broad a range of existing theories as possible, but that you have some idea of where all existing theories are weakest and most need to be supported or changed.

Deciding where you are likely to produce theoretical results which are simple and which predict accurately requires the same sort of guessing as in engineering research, but it is harder here than in engineering research to decide how important the results of a study are likely to be. You must juggle all of these decisions around so as to get the best mix—

a topic which will produce results that are as new and as elegant as possible. This is something for which no rules can be laid down. It is an art.

SETTING OUT A RESEARCH DESIGN It may be true, as I say, that choosing a topic is not something for which rules can be laid down. But it is certainly something for which rules *have* been laid down. Because of an exaggerated fear of *ex post facto* argument, social scientists have developed a very restrictive procedure which one is supposed to use as a standard in carrying on research.[7] According to this procedure, the researcher should first frame a theory, stating it in the form of a set of hypotheses to be tested. These hypotheses presumably are based on work others have done in the past. He should then gather fresh data with which to test the theory. Finally, having tested the theory, he should either reject it or enshrine it, *solely on the basis of those new data.* It is true that this procedure erects formidable barriers to protect us from *ex post facto* argument, but it has a number of serious drawbacks.

In the first place, it lends an exaggerated significance to the results of the new study. Even where a variety of previously existing evidence favors a particular theory, that evidence presumably is to be ignored if the new test gives contradictory results. Moreover, there is a second bad result which is rather more relevant to this chapter. The usual procedure deters researchers from casting about creatively for research topics and theories. Because it requires that hypotheses be fixed firmly at the beginning of the research process, it effectively reduces the researcher to picking obvious hypotheses. It offers him no encouragement to think about his theory at all once he has started his research. He is not supposed to remold his theory as he goes along, learning more about the subject. He is supposed to react to old theories and concepts, rather than think up entirely new problems for explanation. In short, it encourages him to function as a clerk.

This standard for research reaches its peak of rigidity in the "research design"—a common student exercise in which the student is instructed to frame some hypotheses (presumably based on his reading) and show how

---

[7] *Ex post facto* argument results when an investigator forms a theory on the basis of certain evidence, then uses that same evidence to test the theory. If a political scientist formed a theory of Congressional committees on the basis of his intimate experience with the House Appropriations Committee, for example, and then carried out a study of the House Appropriations Committee to test his theory, this would be *ex post facto* argument. The danger in this is that any particular situation usually has certain unique aspects, which are likely to be included in any theory based on it. If that same situation is then used to test the theory, it will look as if the unique aspects are indeed general, whereas if a different situation had been used to test the theory, those parts of the theory would have been found wanting.

he might gather data to test those hypotheses. A doctoral candidate whom I once talked with seemed to me to be the fitting result of repeated exposure to exercises such as these. He needed to find a topic for his dissertation and he thought that a good way to do this would be to look through Lane's *Political Life*, pick a few of Lane's propositions about voting behavior, and test them with some data.

This is how we train people to do research, but most of us have better sense than to follow our own precepts. A search of articles in political science journals will turn up only a few which report research that follows the rules.

One of the better-kept secrets in political science is that good political scientists generally do not draw up research designs before they start to work on a topic. Nor do they usually "frame hypotheses" in any formal sense before they start to work, though they may have some operational hunches about what they expect to find. And they most certainly do not ignore older evidence, even the evidence which suggested a theory to them in the first place.

Their procedure is much less formal than that which they prescribe for students. They play with data, immerse themselves in what other people have written, argue, and think. In doing so, they grope for interesting theories, theories which are elegant and give some sort of a new slant to things.

Actually, following the formal procedure for designing research should not be rejected completely as one of the paths a researcher may follow in this search for interesting theory, but it is only one of many. Sometimes researchers do follow it, and an argument can be made for encouraging students to design their work in the formal manner on the grounds that even though it stifles initiative and creativity, it does have the virtue of being safer and more compact than the more rambling search. Inasmuch as students usually operate under stricter deadlines than other researchers, it makes sense for them to work in such a way that they can estimate accurately at the beginning of a project when they can expect to be finished. Also, it is hard to teach someone to grope for interesting topics and theories. Perhaps a good way for him to learn is by starting with the more clear and obvious procedures, and gradually loosening up as he gains experience.

A MACHIAVELLIAN'S GUIDE TO DEVELOPING RESEARCH TOPICS

There really is no way to set down a procedure by which you can develop a research topic, other than to state as twin goals that you should try to develop a topic which is likely to produce results which are (1) new and (2) elegant. But it may at least help if I set out the problem of developing a topic in a slightly different way at this point.

It has been implicit in this chapter that scholarly research represents a loose cooperative effort among many people. I mentioned earlier the pleasure that researchers feel in creating something that no one has seen before. This is mixed, however, with a pleasure in being part of an ongoing tradition. One's work is something brand new, but it also draws on Karl Marx, or Emile Durkheim, or V. O. Key, and *modifies the meaning of their work*. Scholars involved in developing theory form a kind of a priesthood—admittedly often run less on faith and more according to the laws of laissez-faire and caveat emptor—but still a priesthood focused on the common goal of perfecting elegant theories. As we have seen, the celebrants carry on this process by developing theories and adapting old ones, fitting these theories to the real world to see how accurately they predict things, and feeding the results of such research back into the body of theory.[8]

From this description of the process of research, we can derive a set of rules to guide the individual researcher. If empirical research is motivated by a desire to affect the state of theories, either by confirming them or by working changes in them, then you will be doing your best job when you maximize your effect on theory with a given investment of time and money. In order to do this you must:

(1) *Maximize the Generality of the Theory Which You Are Going to Examine*   I discussed this earlier as a criterion for elegance. Note, though, that this is partly just a matter of how the researcher phrases his problem, for any phenomenon can be examined at different levels of generality. One man may be hit on the head by an apple and form a theory of falling apples; another may have the same experience and form a theory of universal gravitation. The physical activity of the "study" is the same in both cases; the difference lies solely in the level at which the researcher works.

An example of this from political science research may be found in work done on the Presidency. The narrowest range of theory is found in biographies of particular Presidents. The researcher in such a biography generally is concerned only with explaining what happened during the particular President's life, especially during his term in office. A broader range of theory is aimed at in studies of the Presidency in America which analyze the nature of the office, the sources of Presidents' power, the way in which Presidents' personalities can influence their behavior in office, and

---

[8] Needless to say, it is not quite as neat as this. For one thing, a given person usually does not do all of these things himself in a given problem. One person may work simply at clarifying theories, another may do a descriptive study of a particular case, which still another person relates back to the theories. Most researchers can expect to carry on any or all activities at any time.

so on.[9] A still broader range of theory is seen in studies which, in the tradition of Macchiavelli, use the American Presidency as an example of sovereigns in general and seek to explain the sources and limitations of sovereign power. Richard Neustadt's *Presidential Power*, for instance, often operates at this level of generality.[10]

This is too simple, of course. Any one piece of work often operates simultaneously at various levels of generality. A good biography will draw conclusions that apply more broadly than merely to the subject of the biography himself. All I am saying is that, all other things being equal, research which has broad theoretical significance is better than research which has narrow theoretical significance.

(2) *Pick a Weak Theory to Work On*   The weaker the previous confirmations of a theory have been, the greater the likelihood that it will be refuted by your findings. Or if it is confirmed, your findings will be of more importance as evidence for the theory if it was originally weak than if there originally had been a great deal of other evidence confirming it.

Perhaps the best way to use the strategy of picking a weak theory is to state a new, original theory yourself. Then you are obviously in good shape. The theory is automatically weak, inasmuch as there have been no previous tests of it, and thus the evidence you buttress it with will be important. Remember, though, that "new, original theories" which are also elegant are hard to come up with.

Another way to follow this strategy is to pick an anomaly—that is, a question on which previous research has been contradictory. A good example of research stimulated by an anomaly is Sidney Tarrow's study of the political participation of French peasants.[11] Tarrow was struck by the fact that although French peasants regularly responded to surveys by stating that they were not very interested in politics, they also regularly turned out to vote in greater numbers than the urban French.

This led him to probe more deeply into what political involvement means to the French, so as to resolve the apparent contradiction. His conclusions led to the rejection of the old "interest in politics" measure. They also shed new light on the nature of the attachment of French voters to political parties, for that turned out to be the basic cause of the paradox. Anomalies such as this are hard to come by, because earlier investigators generally have noticed them already and have tried to resolve them. But

---

[9] For example, a study of the nature of the Presidential office, such as Koenig, 1968, or a study of presidents' political personalities like Barber, 1972.

[10] Neustadt, 1965.

[11] Tarrow, 1971.

if you can find an anomaly having to do with a significant area of political theory, you can be certain that if you are able to resolve it, your results will be very interesting.

You might also choose a problem in which not enough research has been done to cover all variables which you suspect might be important. You might, for example, replicate a study in a different context than that in which it was first carried out. A group of researchers at the University of Kentucky designed a problem in this way after they noted that political socialization studies of American children had all been carried out in urban, industrialized communities.[12] These studies had shown that children developed favorable views of the government and the President very early in life. The Kentucky group suspected that in more isolated parts of the country, less tied into the national system, children are not taught to support the government in the same way. They designed a study to test this in eastern Kentucky and found that the children there were indeed much more skeptical about the President and government than children had been found to be in the earlier studies.

(3) *Make the Connections Between the General Theory and Your Specific Operations as Clear as Possible*   This really just boils down to making sure you say what you think you are saying. It involves such things as the accuracy of your deductions from the theory to the specific situation, the accuracy with which you have measured things, and so on. Much of the rest of this book is addressed to such problems.

You may have noticed that these three rules resemble the criteria for elegance fairly closely. You also may have noticed that the basic rule behind them—"Do research which makes as big a splash as possible"—reads like a guide for ruthless and hungry assistant professors. But each of the rules which I have derived from the general rule also has a beneficial effect on the field as a whole. If individuals choose those problems of theory which have so far had the weakest verification, for example, this has the effect for the field as a whole of channeling research into theories which are most in need of investigation.

The rules are flexible, providing for different mixes of research strategy which are equally useful in the development of theories. There is no one Scientific Method involved here. One man may find a tool which measures a variable better than had been done before and then simply apply it to sharpen previously examined relationships. Another may note an anomaly in a theory and organize an experiment to resolve the problem. Another may look over previous research findings and place a new, broader or

[12] Jaros, Hirsch, and Fleron, 1968.

simpler, interpretation on them. All are following the rule of maximizing their impact on theory.

Some questions you might consider are:

1. Presumably, work in normative philosophy or in formal theory could be evaluated in terms of "elegance," just as empirical research is. What changes would this require in the definition of "elegance"?

2. This chapter has implied that the usual way to come up with a theory is to focus on a body of observations and look for regular patterns in them. This is the usual way it is done, but it is not the only way and is not necessarily the best. What drawbacks might it involve? In what alternative ways might one develop a theory? (Hint: Think of the distinction between induction and deduction.)

3. I stated in this chapter that most social science theories are causal. What would a noncausal theory look like? Under what circumstances would it be likely to be used? (Hint: Consider Einstein's famous theory, $e = mc^2$.)

THE IMPORTANCE OF DIMENSIONAL THINKING

3

In the preceding chapter I argued that flexibility and originality—in a word, freedom—are important in doing good research. In this chapter I shall stress the need to state theories in a clear, unambiguous way—a form of self-discipline which must accompany that freedom.

I shall concentrate on one particular way to insure clarity. What I shall urge is that you try to state theories in terms of concepts which cannot be subdivided into further distinct meanings, either denotative or connotative. In other words, you should try to compose your theory of very simple concepts whose meaning is clear. Above all, each of these concepts should convey only a single meaning to the reader. I shall call such simple concepts "unidimensional," in contrast to concepts which simultaneously may mean more than one thing, which I shall call "multidimensional." Consider the following example.

As a description of climates, "temperature" is a unidimensional concept. Temperature can vary along only one dimension, from hot to cold. Therefore, if a theory states that a temperature below x degrees causes the spotted ibex to stop breeding, that statement will mean the same thing to every reader. "Good weather," on the other hand, is a multi-dimensional concept describing climates; it involves temperature, wind velocity, humidity, amount of precipitation, degree of cloud cover, and so on. If there is a variation along any one of these separate dimensions, the "goodness" of weather varies. If the theory suggested above stated that "bad weather" caused the spotted ibex to stop breeding, the meaning of that theory would be left to the reader's judgment. Is it rain that discourages the ibex's ardor? Or do high winds make him think of other things? Is it the heat? The humidity?

As in this example, a good general rule is that theories which are framed in terms of unidimensional concepts are better than those which

involve one or more multi-dimensional concepts. The meaning of the one
is clear; the meaning of the other is not. This is the point I shall discuss
in this chapter. Doing so will take us beyond formal statements of the sort
which are usually called "theories." We shall also have to look at the
English language in general, and at the varied "theories" which may be
hidden in ordinary language.

**ENGLISH AS
A LANGUAGE
FOR RESEARCH**

I have assumed above that if political research is
to be useful, a minimal requirement is that its
results should mean the same thing to any two
different readers. Unfortunately, the English language is badly designed to function as a medium
for stating research results clearly and without am-
biguity. Most English words can take on a variety of meanings, depending
on the context and on the mood of the reader. To use an everyday example,
the statement, "The welfare bill failed in the House because the administration did not fight for it," might mean:

1. A welfare bill was passed, but not the one the writer wanted.
2. No welfare bill passed at all.

Whichever of these two is the case, it may have been the result of the
fact that:

3. The administration privately passed the word to its supporters to undercut
   the bill.
4. The administration wanted the bill, but did not work as hard for it as it
   usually does for bills it wants.
5. The administration worked as hard for the bill as it usually does for bills it
   wants, but not as hard as the writer would have done had he been in the
   administration.
6. The administration went all-out for the bill, but failed to get it passed—and
   the writer is in the opposing party.

Note that in these statements there are many additional phrases which are
ambiguous: "passed the word," "undercut the bill," "wanted the bill," "work
hard for the bill," "go all-out."

As an example of a multi-dimensional concept, consider "political
party." This concept can be broken down into at least six component dimensions: those people who vote for the party in a given election, those
people who are registered with the party, those people who "identify"
themselves in their minds with the party, those people who do voluntary
work for the party at some given time, the officers of the party, those who
are running or elected as candidates under the party label. When a polit-

ical scientist writes about "the political party," he may be referring to any or all of these various dimensions of the term. Unless he specifies for the reader which dimensions he means to use, he creates confusion. A few further examples of multi-dimensional terms are: "power," "enjoyment," "conservative," "economic development," "intelligent," and "love."

Time and again, debates in political science resolve themselves into the fact that participants are using the same term in different ways. The official name of the country Americans commonly call "East Germany," for example, is the "German Democratic Republic." Most people in North America and Western Europe do not accept that label. The disagreement originates in the difference between Western and Communist definitions of "democracy." In the West, "democracy" usually is defined by the existence of competing political parties, operating in free elections, with some reasonable level of popular participation in the process. For Communists, who admittedly did not take up the term until after World War II—presumably in order to help legitimize themselves—it has more to do with how the economy is organized; it refers especially to economic equality. Both definitions are implied in the broad and ambiguous concept "democracy." The disagreement stems from the fact that two sides emphasize different aspects of the concept.

The tactic which I introduced earlier, framing theories in terms of unidimensional concepts, can help us to keep clear the meanings of the words we use and to avoid this kind of confusion.

ORDINARY LANGUAGE

As we have seen above, however, many English words involve more than one dimension, and these component dimensions usually are specified only vaguely. Multi-dimensional concepts are valuable and useful in ordinary language, as is indicated by their popularity. The connotations accruing to a word which simultaneously means many different things add richness to our language. Art and rhetoric could not be restricted to unidimensional vocabularies.

But in the social sciences, we pay a high price for this benefit. Rich connotations, which are so important to art, get in the way of analytic thinking. A poet is pleased if a word he uses may mean different things depending on how the reader looks at it; it is his job to create a rich confusion of varied nuances. The job of the social analyst, however, is to reduce confusion to simple theories.

Multi-dimensional words hamper social scientists in at least three ways:

(1) *Because a reader never can be certain in what sense a multi-*

dimensional word was intended, such words make it more difficult for one researcher to communicate his ideas intelligibly to another.

(2) *Whenever a social scientist wants to measure a variable, he is faced with impossible choices unless he has defined the variable in such a way that it consists of a single dimension.* For example, consider a political scientist who wanted to measure the "amount of interaction" between various nations. Now, "interaction" involves a number of dimensions: alliances, amount of trade, tourism, exchanges of mail, and so on. Suppose this political scientist discovered the following things about countries A, B, and C:

Between Countries	Volume Trade/Year	Items of Mail/Year	Alliance
A and B	$1 billion	2 million	Yes
B and C	$½ billion	3 million	Yes
A and C	$2 billion	1 million	No

Between which two countries is there greater interaction? A and C trade together a great deal, but are not allies; B and C exchange a great deal of mail, but do not trade together as much as A and B. Had the investigator defined his variables in terms of single dimensions, he would not have had this problem. In this case, for instance, he might have chosen to use simultaneously three separate, unidimensional variables—trade, mail flow, and alliance. Because these are all single dimensions, which are not reduced into further component parts, each of them can be measured unambiguously. A and C share the greatest trade, for instance, followed by A and B and by B and C. We shall return to such problems of measurement in Chapter 4.

(3) *From the standpoint of the social scientist, another fault in multidimensional words is that each such word is itself a theory of sorts.* By grouping several distinct things under a single term, a multi-dimensional word implies the theory that these things go together. *But, unless its component dimensions are made explicit, it is a poorly articulated and poorly controlled theory.*

For example, the word "wise" has long connoted: (1) broad practical knowledge, (2) a highly developed understanding of relationships, (3) a contemplative bent, and (4) a long background of practical experience. Among other things, it has implied the theory that the older (and thus the more experienced) one got, the better one understood things.

"Theories" such as this, embedded in multi-dimensional words, change as common usage reflects changed moods and new experiences. But the process by which they change is not a very satisfactory one; it is a process which gives us little confidence in the new theories that are produced. It may be an unarticulated dislike for the theory implied by the word "wise," for example, which has led to the diminished use of the word in egalitarian America, and its degradation in such slang as "Don't get wise with me!" and "wise guy." It is in just such a way that word usage gradually changes, reflecting different views of the world. The polite substitution of the term "developing nations" for "underdeveloped countries" in the 1950s and 1960s is another example. This change in usage reflected the changed status of the Third World, and at least some wishful thinking about what was happening there.

This process of "theory development" is uncontrolled. In a sense it is very democratic—probably more democratic than we would like. Everyone who uses the word takes part in the process, and his influence is more or less proportional to the number of people who hear him use the word. There is no provision made for greater influence on the process by those who know more about the subject. Dictionaries, by codifying word usage, serve to slow down the process of change, but they do not affect the *quality* of the change.

Another problem with the process is that these changes often entail enormous lags in time. Theories which are embedded in multi-dimensional words survive practical refutation much longer than would be the case if they were made explicit. The words "liberal" and "conservative" are a good case in point. Because such attitudes as a desire for economic activism on the part of the government, concern for the legal rights of individuals, pacifism, and internationalism often seemed to go together when one looked at the political elite in the United States, the term "liberal" came to denote their presence and "conservative" their absence. (The words were borrowed from the European context, but their meanings were considerably changed, which only added to the subsequent confusion.) The implied theory—that these attitudes tended to coincide—was never very accurate as a description of the elite and it has proved to be quite inaccurate in describing people in general.[1] It turns out, for example, that people who are "liberal" on individuals' rights are often "conservative" on economic issues. All this went unnoticed until at least the late forties, and there are still many people who use the words "liberal" and "conservative" in this way, as if they had general validity.

Thus, while changes in usage do produce changes in the theories implied by multi-dimensional words, the process by which these changes are made is capricious; this is presumably not the way we want to develop

[1] A good demonstration of this—there are dozens—is Converse, 1964.

social theory. A social scientist should not hide away in his statement of a theory additional little theories which are implicit and uncontrolled.

Let me sum up the argument so far: It is important for social scientists to use unidimensional language for three reasons:

1. The meaning of a theory is not unambiguously clear if it is couched in multi-dimensional words;
2. Variables cannot be measured unambiguously if they have been defined in a multi-dimensional way;
3. Inclusion of multi-dimensional words in a theory confuses that theory with additional theories which are implied by the existence of the multi-dimensional words themselves.

At the same time, however, the English language contains, and should contain, many words which hold a rich variety of meanings and connotations.

As a result of all this, social scientists often must create their own vocabulary. If ordinary language does not provide unidimensional words for the things a social scientist wants to say, he must himself make up the words he needs. This is one reason why social science writing so often strikes readers as flat and cold. What most people mean by "social science jargon" is simply the unidimensional vocabulary invented by social scientists for their use in analytic research.

Writing from which the richness of varied connotations has been removed is flat. This is simply one of the costs we must pay in order to write analytically. Of course, this is not meant to excuse poor writing in the social sciences or anywhere else. Unidimensional language is a minor handicap under which the social scientist operates, but it need not prevent him from writing clear and graceful prose.

Actually, writers in any analytic field suffer the same handicap. Natural scientists must create their own vocabularies, too. But somehow the loss of richness seems more painful in the social sciences than in other fields. The physicist may describe a body's motion in terms of "mass," "velocity," and "acceleration," rather than saying that it "hurtles through space," and the mind does not rebel. But when the political scientist describes politics as consisting of "system inputs," "system outputs," and "feedback loops," the mind does rebel. This is because the social scientist deals with *people*, the thing we care most passionately about. It does not bother us when a physicist tries to reduce the complex motion of a particle to unidimensional concepts, but it does bother us when social scientists try to do this to the complex reality of politics, or of the family, or of protests, or whatever.

THE PROPER USE OF MULTI-DIMENSIONAL WORDS

I have argued that we should try to use only indivisible dimensions as concepts in political science. But there is another side to the question, which leads me to temper that stance somewhat. Though it is always necessary to think and work with unidimensional concepts in the social sciences, it may be convenient to put separate dimensions together in *explicit* multi-dimensional combinations.

"National integration" may provide an example of such a concept. There are many dimensions implied in the term: political consensus within the nation; widespread communication and personal interchanges within the nation; a feeling, among the nation's people, that they all belong together; legal integration; and so on. It would be possible to do without the term "national integration," and work directly with these dimensions, but it would be very awkward. There are a great number of dimensions involved, and they may combine in odd ways. At the same time, there *is* a widespread feeling among political scientists that these things tend to go together to constitute a general process. This process might not be at all easy to discern if we were forced to work simultaneously with the large number of unidimensional concepts involved in it. Accordingly, political scientists over the last few decades have developed the term "national integration," *explicitly* composed of these various dimensions, to refer to the general process. The result has not been fully satisfactory, but there does appear to be a need for such a summary term.

The use of an explicit combination of separate dimensions such as this has some of the advantages of both "ordinary language" and unidimensional language, and some of the disadvantages of each. Such summary constructs may add grace and interest to the presentation of your results and ideas. They may add clarity, too, if you are working with so many dimensions simultaneously that readers would have difficulty keeping track of them.

Such explicit combinations of dimensions have the advantage, as compared with ordinary language, that you have built your own juxtaposition of dimensions into the word. But they retain many of the disadvantages of ordinary language. A reader cannot tell, for example, when faced with a high score on a variable which combines dimensions A, B, and C, whether this means that A and B were high and C low, or that B was high and A and C were low, or whatever. Though explicit multi-dimensional words are more useful than ordinary language, you should not use them casually.

I have used as my "bad" examples words from ordinary language, rather than words specifically designed for use by scholars. In general, as I have indicated, when scholars design terminology it is a good deal tighter than ordinary language. However, even scholarly vocabulary is often not as tight as it could be. It often happens, for instance, that several scholars working independently of each other devise related unidimensional words, each set up for one particular research use. When these related words are taken as a group, they may produce confusion as great as as that resulting from ordinary language. Kroeber and Kluckhohn once counted several hundred different ways in which the word "culture" was used by anthropologists.[2]

Accordingly, explicit dimensional analysis of a body of scholarly work, even that which is already at a quite abstract level, can help us to clarify the meaning of the whole body of work, and may point up new directions for theoretical development. The following analysis of different words used to describe electoral changes is an extended example of how such dimensional analysis might proceed.

An Example of Dimensional Analysis   The classification of electoral changes in American elections dates back to the work of V. O. Key, Jr. In 1955 he pointed to the existence of a certain type of election in which major and lasting realignments occurred.[3] He defined this so-called *critical election* as one in which: "the depth and intensity of electoral involvement are high, in which more or less profound readjustments occur in the relations of power within the community, and in which new and durable electoral groupings are formed."[4] He gave convincing evidence that the 1928 election, at least in New England, had been a critical election.

A few years later, he identified a more gradual type of electoral change, which he called *secular realignment;* this type of change was defined as "a movement of the members of a population category from party to party that extends over several presidential elections and appears to be independent of the peculiar factors influencing the vote at individual elec-

[2] Kroeber and Kluckhohn, 1952.

[3] Key, 1955.

[4] *Ibid.*, p. 4. Note that even though Key designed this concept explicitly, he designed it in multiple dimensions. It can be broken down to three dimensions: intensity of electoral involvement, extent of readjustments in relations of power, and durability of the new groupings.

tions."[5] Again he provided a number of examples from New England. Figure 3–1 gives an example from Key's articles of each type of electoral change.

After Key, a number of political scientists have added to the general pool of election types. The authors of *The American Voter* have added the *maintaining election, the deviating election,* and the *realigning election.* The first is an election "in which the pattern of partisan attachments prevailing in the preceding period persists and is the primary influence on forces governing the vote."[6] In other words, there is no important change. The second is an election in which "the basic division of partisan loyalties is not seriously disturbed, but the attitude forces on the vote are such as to bring about the defeat of the majority party."[7] In other words, a deviating election is one in which there is a shift in voting, but in which the shift is due to short-term factors, not to a realignment in basic sympathies; the previous pattern of voting can soon be expected to reassert itself. And the third is essentially the same as Key's "critical election."[8]

Gerald Pomper has added another category, the *converting election,* to describe an election in which there is a lasting shift in many voters' sympathies, but in which the party which was dominant before the shift continues to be dominant after the shift.[9] This might occur, for example, if the deep South were to shift to the Republicans while a shift of the Midwest to the Democrats compensated for it.

Let me summarize the above classifications:

1. Critical election: an election in which there is great involvement, and in which a lasting realignment of voting patterns occurs.
2. Secular realignment: a gradual process by which a lasting realignment of voting patterns occurs.
3. Maintaining election: an election in which underlying party attachments do not change and voting patterns are much as in the previous election.
4. Deviating election: an election in which underlying party attachments do not change, but in which something distinct to that election (Eisenhower's candidate-appeal, for example, or a recession) causes voters to cast their ballots in unusual ways. There may be a major change in such an election, but the change is not a lasting one, for the old, unchanged party attachments reassert themselves once the transient influence disappears.
5. Realigning election: a critical election.

[5] Key, 1959, p. 199.

[6] Campbell *et al.*, 1960, p. 531.

[7] *Ibid.*, p. 532.

[8] *Ibid.*, p. 534.

[9] Pomper, 1967, esp. pp. 536–38.

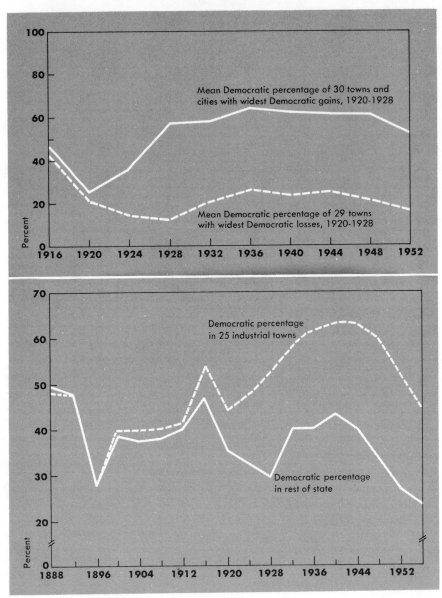

Figure 3–1   Examples of Critical and Secular Change

A. A Critical Election, Massachusetts 1928: Persistence of electoral cleavage, showing mean Democratic percentage of presidential vote in towns with sharpest Democratic gains, 1920–1928, and in towns of widest Democratic losses, 1920–1928.

B. Secular Change, New Hampshire 1904–1936: Democratic percentage of two-party presidential vote in 25 New Hampshire industrial towns and in rest of state, 1888–1956. The values shown for 1912 are the Democratic percentage of the three-party vote; for 1924, the Democratic vote plus the Progressive vote as a percentage of the three-party vote.

Sources: V. O. Key, Jr., "A Theory of Critical Elections," Journal of Politics, XVII (1955), 3–18; and "Secular Realignment of the Party System," Journal of Politics, XXI (1959), 198–210.

6. Converting election: a critical election in which compensating changes occur, so that there is no change in the relative advantage of one party over another, even though large numbers of voters have moved between the parties.

These classifications can be made more useful by clarifying just what they are meant to describe and analyzing the dimensions implied in the various classifications.

First of all, it appears that the emphasis has changed subtly from Key's time to the present, from classifying electoral changes in general to classifying results of particular elections. Certainly Key was concerned in his two articles with a typology of electoral changes. "Secular realignment," for example, would be of no importance and would go undetected in a single election, for it consists of repeated slight shifts over a series of several elections.

But later classifiers have thought in terms of classifying particular elections. For example, the title of the relevant section of *The American Voter* is "A Classification of Presidential Elections." And Pomper's addition to *The American Voter* classification scheme obviously applies only to a particular election. This change in the emphasis of election studies probably is due to the impact of sample surveys as a tool in studying elections. By its nature (largely because of the expense of repeating a survey of the same respondents from one election to the next), the sample survey is best suited to the study of a single election, or at most a series of a few elections. Because researchers using survey data could not easily study whole processes of changes, their thinking apparently switched to dealing primarily with changes involving one or two elections. In the process, Key's "critical elections" article has become a classic in the field, and his "secular change" article remains virtually his least-known piece of work.[10]

Though valuable new ways were developed for looking at changes from one election to the next, much was lost in the switch.[11] First of all, it became more difficult to handle a change which took place over a couple of elections, such as the New Deal realignment, which appears to have proceeded in an irregular process from 1924 to 1936. More importantly, from the point of view of electoral theory, "secular change" dropped out

[10] In the last few years there has been a trend toward reestablishing gradual processes of change in electoral theory. This has come about primarily as a result of increased interest in studying actual voting returns (as Key had done), and also partly from an increased interest in European elections. An example of the better work along these lines is Butler and Stokes, 1969, esp. Chapters 5 and 11.

[11] The contribution of *The American Voter* to an understanding of electoral change was, of course, immense. By applying the psychological variables developed in their survey studies to Key's discussion of critical elections, its authors were able to provide, for the first time, a partial explanatory theory of critical elections— something that Key, despite the title of his paper, could not do.

as an item of concern, despite the fact that many important electoral changes—for instance, the rise of socialist parties in Western Europe—have been of this type.

Pomper's addition of "converting election" to the roster of concepts was another result of looking at particular elections arther than at electoral changes in general. It is appropriate to the analysis of specific elections— for we are accustomed in dealing with an election to ask immediately, "Who won?"—but from the standpoint of a theory of electoral change, it is irrelevant. What is of interest in such a theory is not whether a switch of x percent of the voters pushes a party over 50 percent; rather, we are interested in the shift itself, and the process by which it occurred.

All this is not to say that concepts designed to handle specific elections are in some way unsatisfactory. I just mean to point out that when you are engaged in a research problem you should think hard about whether a given body of concepts is appropriate to what you want to do. I have suggested above that if we want to study electoral change, some review of the usual concepts is required. A convenient way to do this—as is often the case—is to go back to the basic dimensions of the concepts in general use.

Some Dimensions of Electoral Change   Obviously there are infinitely many dimensions which one *could* choose to include. But if we are to keep to the rule of formulating theories which are as simple as possible, we must try to limit ourselves to a relatively small number. I have suggested above that the dimension introduced by Pomper (whether or not same party remains dominant after a change) is unnecessary in the study of election changes, so we shall drop it at the start.

The first dimension which we would have to include is the *magnitude* of a change. Simply, how much change is there? It is certainly the first characteristic of an electoral change which we would wish to explain. Why did a change occur (or not occur) under the circumstances? Why was it as great (or slight) as it was?

A second dimension which we might want to include is the *speed* with which a change took place. This is suggested by Key's distinction between critical elections and secular changes.

Third, we might include the *duration* of a change. How long does the new pattern which resulted from the change last? Like the preceding dimension, this one is suggested by the existing literature—in this case, the distinction drawn by the authors of *The American Voter* between deviating elections and realigning elections. But it suggests, also, the possibility that some new alignments may be more fragile than others.

Using these three dimensions, we can reconstruct the original set of election types (with Pomper's excluded). First of all, if "magnitude" is low,

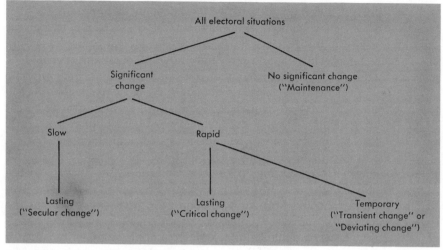

Figure 3–2   Varieties of Electoral Situation

we do not need to examine the change further. All such electoral situations may be labeled "maintaining." [12]

This leaves us with four subtypes of electoral change which are not "maintaining." These correspond to varying combinations of the dimensions "speed" and "duration": slow/temporary, slow/lasting, rapid/temporary, and rapid/lasting. "Slow/temporary" can be eliminated automatically, because a change which takes a considerable time to occur cannot be considered temporary. By the time it has been completed, it has already lasted quite a while. Of the three remaining: (1) "slow/lasting" corresponds to Key's "secular change"; (2) "rapid/temporary" corresponds to a "deviating election" in *The American Voter* scheme; and (3) "rapid/lasting" corresponds to Key's "critical election" and *The American Voter's* "realigning election." The use of the three dimensions to form a basis for the classic typologies is summarized in Figure 3–2.

In my discussion thus far, and in Figure 3–2, I have simplified the three dimensions by treating them as dichotomies (significant/not significant, slow/rapid, and lasting/temporary). I have done this to emphasize the correspondence between the set of dimensions and the various typologies. But one advantage of dimensional thinking is that it reminds us of the continua on which our often more pedestrian thinking is based. In Chapter

[12] Note that I refer to "electoral situations," not "elections." Remember that we can look at either a single election or a whole era of elections in terms of change. It is processes of change we wish to classify, not particular events.

5, I shall present different types of measurement in more detail, but it is clear that a certain amount of information must be sacrificed to squeeze these dimensions into dichotomies. "Speed of change," for example, encompasses more possibilities than "slow" and "rapid." Potentially, it could be measured much more precisely than that, and we would be wasting information to treat the dimension as the dichotomy implied in typologies of elections. As one result of such a dimensional analysis, accordingly, we might decide to ignore the typologies with which we started and work directly with the more basic dimensions: magnitude, speed, and duration.

In the example I have been using, the three dimensions give us a sufficient coverage of the variables needed to characterize electoral changes. In working them out, it was necessary to clarify quite precisely what it was that we wanted to study. And we were then able to specify what was the most economic set of distinct variables for us to use. By keeping these variables distinct, we were reminded of possible combinations and a range of variation not originally involved in the typologies with which we were working. Such a dimensional analysis of the existing literature is often a good way to begin your own work on a problem, particularly if that literature is large.

FURTHER DISCUSSION   An excellent formal treatment of dimensional analysis is Allan H. Barton, "The Concept of Property-Space in Social Research" (1955). Philip E. Jacob's "A Multi-Dimensional Classification of Atrocity Stories" (1955) furnishes a good example of dimensional analysis.

Some examples from political science are: the third chapter of Robert Dahl's *Modern Political Analysis* (1970), which presents the concept "power" and breaks it down into simpler dimensions; Chapter 11 of Dahl's *Political Oppositions in Western Democracies* (1966), a first-rate analysis of the relevant dimensions for classifying "opposition"; Harry Eckstein's *Pressure Group Politics* (1960), pp. 15–40, in which he classifies pressure group activities; and the third chapter of his *Division and Cohesion in Democracy* (1966), an excellent dimensional analysis of "political division." Eckstein, in particular, stands out among political scientists for his thorough and creative handling of concepts and their underlying dimensions.

Finally, as an exercise, you might consider the conceptual problems involved in the well-worn aphorism by Lord Acton: "Power tends to corrupt and absolute power corrupts absolutely."

PROBLEMS OF MEASUREMENT ACCURACY

4

In this chapter I shall explore problems of accurate measurement. These are problems which come up in relating the actual operations in a piece of research—that is, measurements of things—to the concepts which comprise the theory to which the research is supposed to relate. These concepts exist only in the mind. One necessary assumption, if we are to claim that a piece of research has tested a given theory, is that the things measured in the research correspond to the things in the theorist's mind.

This is often a difficult assumption to make. In the preceding chapter, you saw one instance of a problem which might stand in the way of making such an assumption. The political scientist who wanted to measure the amount of interaction between nations found that there was no single indicator which measured "interaction" satisfactorily. A number of things—trade, mail exchanges, alliance, and so on—partook of "interaction," but no one of them alone was exactly what he was thinking of. His problem, therefore, was to measure a concept for which there existed no simple, direct indicator.

In the social sciences, only rarely are we able to measure directly the concepts we use in a theory. Such concepts as "social class," "respect for the President," and "power in the community" cannot be measured directly. The fact that we generally must carry on research using measures which correspond only indirectly to the concepts in our theories comprises the basic problem of measurement in the social sciences.

Consider the concept "social status." In common usage among social scientists there are two popular versions of this concept: "subjective social status," the class an individual considers himself to belong to; and "objective social status," an individual's rank with regard to prestige along social hierarchies such as education, income, and occupation. Neither version of the concept can be measured directly.

In the case of "subjective social status," we cannot measure what the person feels about his status directly. We know what he tells us he feels. But what he tells us he feels may not be what we want. He might not know what he "really" feels, for instance; or he might misunderstand the question and give a misleading answer; or he might feel differently from one day to the next, in which case the measure of his status will depend on the accident of which day we choose to ask him.

In the case of "objective social status," again we cannot measure the variable directly. "Objective status" has something to do with income, something to do with education, something to do with occupation, and something to do with various other hierarchies, some of which we may not know about. None of these provides a sufficient measure in itself. For example, if we tried to use occupation alone as a measure of social status, we would be faced with the embarrassing question of whether a plumber who made $20,000 a year was really of lower social status than a typist who made $7,000 a year. Similarly, if we tried to use income alone as a measure, we would be faced with the problem of what to do with a retired teacher, whose income might be below the poverty level. "Social status" in this case is a concept which is related to a number of measurable things, but is related only imperfectly to each of them. The best we can do in measuring it is to combine the various measurable indicators into a pooled measure which is roughly related to the concept "objective social status."

We encounter similar problems in measuring the other concepts I have cited as examples. Like many other variables in political science, these are concepts which are of considerable interest and use in theories, but which are by their nature impossible to measure. The general problem posed by such variables is presented schematically in Figure 4–1.

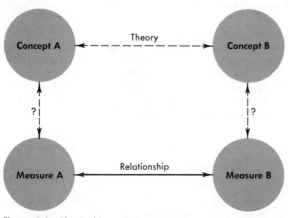

Figure 4–1   The Problem of Measurement

As you saw in Chapter 2, in political research we are commonly interested in relating concepts through a theory. This is always true in theory-oriented research, and it is often true in engineering research as well. If we cannot measure directly the concepts we wish to use, then we find ourselves in the position depicted in Figure 4–1. We want to say, "Concept A bears a relationship of thus-and-so form to Concept B." But all that we can observe is the relationship between Measure A and Measure B. Whether what we say about the measures is an accurate statement of the relationship between the concepts depends on what sort of relationship there is between Concept A and Measure A, and between Concept B and Measure B. We can only guess what these relationships are. Like the theory itself, the relationships cannot be observed.

As an example, suppose you wanted to assess the theory that countries which are increasing their armaments tend to engage in aggressive international policies. You might be faced with the following relationships:

1. *Relationship between the concept 'increasing armaments" and the measure of "increasing armaments."* You clearly cannot measure increases in a nation's armaments directly; only a national intelligence apparatus has the facilities to do that. Therefore, you may take as your measure the country's reported expenditures on armaments. Now, a country which is not preparing to launch an aggressive military venture would have less reason to lie about an arms buildup than would a country (such as Germany in 1933) which was consciously preparing for aggression. Therefore, the relationship between concept and measure in this case might be: When a country is building up its armaments for reasons other than a conscious preparation for aggression, its reported expenditures on arms will increase; when a country is not building up its armaments, or when it is building them up in order to launch an aggressive action, its reported expenditures on arms will not increase.

2. *Relationship between the concept "increasing armaments" and the concept "aggressive international policies."* Let us assume, for this example, that countries which are increasing their armaments tend to engage in aggressive international policies.

3. *Relationship between the concept "aggressive international policies" and the measure of "aggressive international policies."* Let us assume, for this example, that we are able to develop a measure which corresponds almost perfectly to the concept "aggressive international policies." (In practice, of course, this would be a difficult variable to measure, and it certainly would be necessary first to analyze the varied dimensions involved in "aggression" and "policies" to state more clearly just what was meant by the concept.)

We would now find ourselves in the position depicted in Figure 4–2. Thus, because of peculiarities in the relationships between the concepts and the measures of these concepts, the relationship which you can observe between the measures might be the opposite of the true relationship between the concepts. Worse yet, inasmuch as the two measures and the connection

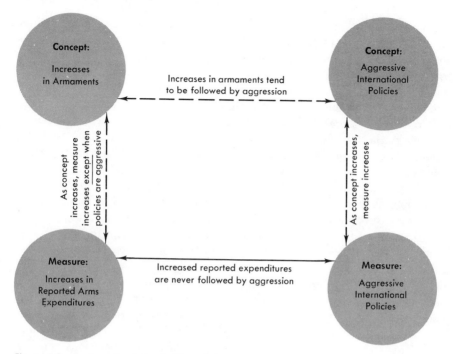

Figure 4–2   An Example of the Problem of Measurement

between them are all that you can observe, you would have no way of knowing that this was happening. This is why I have called indirect measurement of concepts *the* problem of measurement.

One solution to the problem might be to measure variables only directly. Some concepts are directly measurable. A few examples are: people's votes, if an election is nonsecret and you tabulate the result yourself; statements you hear made on the Senate floor; a bomb which you see dropped or thrown.[1]

The difficulty with such a solution is that concepts which can be measured directly are usually trivial in and of themselves. They are too idiosyncratic to use in general, interesting theories. I would hate to say that particular statements by senators lead nowhere, but as far as political theory is concerned, it is true. Any given statement can apply only to itself. It takes on a general meaning only if it is placed in a category, so that it can be

---

[1] It is reasonable, also, to include here reliable observers' accounts of such events. Even though the measurement of these things is technically indirect if you accept another observer's account of them, you should be able to achieve a very tight fit between the concept "event happens" and the measure "reliable observer says that event happens."

compared with other statements. For instance, Senator _____'s statement: "The President's policies are bankrupting the people of my state" is not intrinsically of theoretical interest. It can be placed in various categories, however: "statements of opposition to the President," "statements of concern for constituents' needs," "bombastic statements." Placing it in one of these categories allows us to compare it with other senatorial statements and to develop theories about the causes and effects of such statements.

Note, though, that by placing it into a category we have used the statement as an indirect measure of the concept which the category represents. No given statement is a perfect case of the "bombastic statement" or of the "statement of opposition to the President." Rather, a number of statements *approximate* each category, and we choose to use those statements as indirect measures of the abstract concept which we cannot measure.

To sum up the argument so far: in order for a concept to be useful in building theories, it usually must be an abstraction, which cannot be measured directly. Further, of those interesting concepts which *are* in principle directly measurable (how individuals vote in an election, for example), many cannot be measured directly for practical reasons (the elections are held with a secret ballot). Therefore, most of the time we must work with variables which are indirect measures of the concepts in which we are interested. This means that there is interposed, between our operations and the theory we want to work on, the relationships between our concepts and their measures. This is the situation illustrated graphically in Figures 4–1 and 4–2. The chief problem of measurement is to insure, as much as possible, that the relationships between concepts and measures are such that the relationship between the measures mirrors the relationship between the concepts.

Problems we may encounter in trying to achieve this correspondence between measures and concepts fall under two headings—problems of measure *reliability* and problems of measure *validity*.

RELIABILITY

A measure is reliable to the extent that it gives the same result again and again if the measurement is repeated. For example, if a person is asked several days in a row whether he is married, and his answers vary from one day to the next, the measure of his marital state is unreliable. If his answers are stable from one time to the next, the measure is reliable.

The analogy of measuring with a yardstick may help make the meaning of reliability clear. An ordinary wooden yardstick will give approximately the same length each time, if the same object is measured with it a number of times. If the yardstick were made of an elastic material, its results would not be so reliable. It might say that a chair was twenty inches high one day, sixteen the next. Similarly, if it were made of a material that expanded or contracted greatly with changes in temperature, its results would not be reliable. On hot days it would say that the chair was shorter than on cold days. In fact, the choice of wood as a material for yardsticks is in part a response to the problem of reliability in measurement, a problem certainly not confined to the social sciences. Wood is cheap, rigid, and relatively unresponsive to changes in temperature.

There are many sources of unreliability in social science data. The sources vary, depending on what kinds of data are used. Official statistics, for example, may be unreliable because of an unusual number of clerical errors or because of variability in how categories are defined from one time to the next. ("Votes cast in an election," for instance, may mean "all votes, including spoiled ballots" at one time, "all valid votes" at another.) Attitude measures may be unreliable because a question is hard for respondents to understand, and they interpret it one way at one time, another way the next. Or the people punching responses onto cards may make mistakes.

As an illustration, let us list the various sources of unreliability that might be involved in the example I used above, in which asking whether the respondent was married yielded results which were not stable over time:

1. The question might be phrased badly, so that respondents sometimes interpreted it to mean "Are you now married?" and sometimes "Have you ever been married?"
2. Respondents might be playing games with the interviewer, answering questions randomly.
3. Dishonest interviewers might be playing games with the researcher by filling out the forms themselves instead of going to the trouble of getting the respondents to answer them.
4. Respondents' answers might depend on their mood. Perhaps they would answer "yes" when they had had a good day, "no" when they had had a bad day.
5. Respondents' answers might depend on the context of the interview. A man might say "no" to attractive women, "yes" to everyone else.
6. There might be simple clerical errors in copying down the answers, either by the interviewer on the spot or by the card-puncher who transcribes the interviewers' copy onto data cards.

Admittedly, many of these possibilities are far-fetched. The example itself is a bit strained, inasmuch as straightforward informational items like this one usually can be measured with reasonable reliability. But the same sorts of conditions affect the reliability of less straightforward survey questions, such as "What do you like about candidate X?" "What social class do you consider yourself to be a member of?" and "Do you feel people generally can be trusted?"

So far, I have treated the unreliability of a measure as if it were a result of unpredictability in the relationship between the concept and its measure. An additional source of unreliability in the measure is variability in the "true value" of the concept itself. In the example above, a further source of unreliability might be the simple fact that some people got married or got divorced from one time to the next. This would be easily distinguishable from other sources of unreliability, for it would show up as a recognizable pattern of stable answers up to a certain point, followed by changed, but once again stable, answers.

A more interesting variability in the "true value" may occur, however, when the "true value" varies randomly. This situation sometimes provides the basis for interesting theories. Converse, for instance, has noted that on many standard questions of political policy, people's attitudes appear to vary randomly across time.[2] He concludes that on certain issues, the mass public simply does not form stable opinions; and he goes on to draw interesting comparisons between elite and mass opinion, based on that conclusion.

Note that, in order to reach this conclusion, he has to assume that he has effectively eliminated other sources of unreliability, such as interviewer error and confusion about the meaning of questions. Having first eliminated these sources of unpredictability in the relationship between concept and measure, he then can treat the unreliability in his measure as a reflection of unreliability in the concept.

Although unreliability sometimes may be of theoretical interest in its own right, as it is in this case, it usually is a barrier to our research, which we want to eliminate. Careful work is the best way to achieve reasonable reliability—double-checking all clerical work, trying out the questionnaire on a small pilot study in order to catch and correct unclear questions, and so on.

We often wish to know how successfully we have reduced unreliability. A number of tests have been developed, which can be used to check the reliability of a measure. I shall mention two of them briefly, to give you an idea of what can be done.

The so-called *test-retest check for reliability* simply consists of repeating the measurement a second time, with a suitable length of time falling

[2] Converse, 1964.

between the two measurements. If the second measure tends strongly to be the same as the first measure—that is, if the measure is stable over the elapsed time—the measure is considered relatively reliable. One problem with this test, of course, is that there is no way to distinguish instability which is due to "real" unreliability in the concept being measured from instability which is due to problems in the measurement process.

Another test, the *split-half check for reliability,* avoids this problem. It is appropriate whenever a measure consists of a group of items which are to be combined to form the measure—for instance, a measure of "social status," which is made by combining such items as individuals' income, occupation, education, house size, and neighborhood into a single summary measure; or a measure of "welfare policy expenditures," which groups budget items such as welfare payments, unemployment relief, hospital subsidies, and school lunch programs into a single summary measure.

In the split-half test, the researcher divides these assorted items into two groups and then composes a summary "measure" out of each of the groups. Because all of the items are taken to be measures of the same thing, the two summary measures should tend to be the same. A measure of how close they are to each other provides a check on how reliable the total summary measure is.

As an example, consider a measure of "welfare policy expenditures" by states, which combines expenditures on a variety of items, all of them more or less having to do with "welfare policy." It might be that one particular item—disaster relief, for instance—varies greatly from state to state and from one year to the next in any one state. In one year there might be no natural disasters; in another there might be floods or a hurricane. That particular item would be a source of unreliability in the overall measure. It also should cause the split-half test to show a relatively low reliability, for its erratic variation would make the score based on the group in which it was included less likely to equal the score based on the group which did not include it.

These two checks for reliability complement each other. The test-retest check is appropriate for any sort of measure which can be repeated. It checks for *all* sources of unreliability, but this often includes changes in the "true value" of the concept, rather than only the instability that is due to the measurement process.

The split-half check is appropriate for measures which are made up of a composite of subitems. It checks only for those sources of unreliability which do not operate over time, inasmuch as all of the subitems presumably are measured at the same time. Accordingly, it may miss some sources of instability in the measurement process, such as the effect of the length of time since payday or of changes in the weather, on respondents' answers to an interview question. But it derives an important benefit from this, because one of the sources of instability screened out is true change over time in the concept, which you might not wish to confuse with instability due to the measurement process.

VALIDITY

Reliability has to do with how dependably a measure mirrors its concept. In thinking about reliability, it is assumed that the measure *tends* to mirror the concept faithfully and that the problem of reliability is simply that this tendency may be a rather loose one. It is assumed, in other words, that if the concept were measured a large number of times, the average of those measures would mirror the concept faithfully. The problem is that any one of those measures may be rather far from the true value of the concept. In terms of Figures 4–1 and 4–2, it is assumed that the relationship between concept and measure is one of equivalence; the problem is that that relationship may be rather weak.

A second general problem, distinct from reliability, is the problem of *validity*. A measure is valid if it tends to mirror the concept truly. That is, whether or not a measure is reliable, if there is an equivalence relationship between it and its concept, the measure is valid.[3] A measure can be valid and yet not be reliable. Or, it can be reliable and yet not be valid. If it gives the same result repeatedly, the measure is reliable, but it may distort the concept in the same way each of these times, so that it does not tend to mirror it faithfully.

The relationship between the measure "increases in reported arms expenditures" and the concept "increases in armaments" in Figure 4–2 is an example of invalid measurement. The relationship between the concept and the measure is such that, when "increases in armaments" are high, "increases in reported arms expenditures" may be either high or low, depending on the reason for the arms buildup. The measure might be reliable (a country which reported low increases in one year, for instance, should be likely to report low increases the next year also), but it would still be invalid, because the relationship between the concept and the measure is not such that the measure accurately mirrors the concept.

To sum up, a measure is *reliable*—whether or not it faithfully measures the concept it is meant to measure—if it is stable when it is repeated. A measure is *valid*—no matter how stable it is under repetition—if, in the long or short run, it tends to measure the concept it is meant to measure.

---

[3] I have departed from common usage here. Most authors define "invalidity" as any lack of correspondence between concept and measure, *including* a lack of correspondence due to unreliability. Thus, for a measure to be valid, it must tend to mirror the concept truly, and must also be reliable. In my experience, however, students have not found the common usage helpful, since it provides no distinct category for a measure which tends to mirror truly, but does so unreliably.

A few examples are in order. There are many ways that a measure can be invalid.

One common source of invalid measures is extrapolation from a sample to a population which is not really represented by the sample. Using letters to the editor as an indicator of public opinion would be unwise, for instance, because the people who write those letters are not an accurate cross-section of the public as a whole. Their opinions would not be a valid measure of "public opinion."

A comic case of sampling problems from the early days of opinion polls is the *Literary Digest* poll. The *Literary Digest* was a giant magazine in the United States in the early part of this century. Starting in 1924, the *Digest* ran an ambitious poll in Presidential election years. Virtually everyone who owned a car or a telephone was reached by the poll, which was sent out to a mailing list obtained from telephone directories and state automobile registration lists. Only about 20 percent of the sample ballots mailed out were returned, but even at that, the *Digest* had over 2 million responses each time.

The *Digest* sample distorted the United States population in two ways. First of all, it essentially sampled only the upper and middle classes, inasmuch as those who did not have a car or a telephone—at a time when cars and telephones were far less universally owned than today—did not get onto the mailing list. Also, it only sampled those who were interested enough and energetic enough to return the sample ballot. With only 20 percent of those who received the ballot returning it, this seems to have been a rather select sample.

In 1924, 1928, and 1932, the *Digest* poll was very successful, coming within a few percentage points of the actual outcome in each of those elections. By 1932 the poll had become an institution; it was attacked in the *Congressional Record* and featured in *New Yorker* cartoons.

In 1936, the poll predicted Landon by a landslide. When the *Literary Digest* went out of business the next year, it was thought that the shock and loss of reputation from having called the election so badly was a factor in the magazine's demise.

Apparently the interested, middle-class sample which the *Digest* used did not vote much differently than the rest of the country from 1924 through 1932. Accordingly, its sympathies were a valid measure of the way the country was going to vote in those elections. Between 1932 and 1936, however, Roosevelt initiated the New Deal, which broadened his support among the poor and drove the middle class to the Republicans. After 1936, the sympathies of the middle class were no longer a valid measure of the way the country would vote.

Another way to construct an invalid measure is to ask people a question which means something different to them than what you had intended. It had always been thought, for example, that farmers in France tended to be apolitical. When asked "How interested are you in politics?" they had generally responded, "Not at all." At the same time, it was striking that voting participation was higher among farmers than among most groups in the French population. If they were not interested in politics, why did they vote?

In his study designed to explore this paradox, which I cited as an example in Chapter 2, Sidney Tarrow discovered that the innocent question about political interest had been spreading confusion. French farmers apparently interpreted "interest in politics" to mean commitment to some particular party, which many of them vehemently rejected. Thus, many farmers who were interested in politics but considered themselves independents responded "Not at all" to this invalid measure of "interest in politics."

CHECKING FOR VALIDITY

Taking Precautions   Our problem in checking the validity of a measure is similar to the general problem of measurement, depicted in Figure 4–1. We say that a measure is valid if the relationship between it and its concept is such that the measure faithfully mirrors the concept. *But the general problem of measurement is precisely the fact that usually all we can observe is the measures.* We cannot know what the relationship between a concept and its measure is. How, then, can we assess the validity of the measure?

The answer, of course, is that there is no pat way to do so. Part of the "craft" in the craft of political research is cleverness and care in developing measures which appear likely to be valid. There are two main strategies to follow in developing valid measures.

The first consists simply of taking precautions against invalidity while constructing a measure. It sounds deceptively simple, but the most important thing is to think through the measurement process carefully. You should try to think of ways in which the relationship between concept and measure might be a distorting one and then take precautions against that happening.

For example, we now know that drawing a sample in certain ways (drawing a random sample, for instance) guards against a fiasco like that which destroyed the *Literary Digest* poll. As another example, in testing out a questionnaire which you hope to use in a study, you might well ask a few people to answer your questions and afterward ask them what they thought the questions meant as they answered them. This may alert you to questions which mean something different to your respondents than they mean to you.

These two examples simply require that the investigator think ahead to problems that could occur in the relationship between concept and measure, and that he act either to prevent these or to check to see whether they are present. At the most general level, the "strategy" I have suggested here requires only that the investigator consider carefully whether he can honestly believe that the measure mirrors the concept.

A Test of Validity   The "strategy" above did not actually provide a test of the validity of the measure. Such a test can be made, however, although it is of necessity subjective and open to varying interpretations. Let us say that we want to decide whether measure α is a valid measure of concept A. If there is some measure β that we are certain is strongly related to concept A, then we can check to see whether measure β is related to measure α. If it is not, then α must not be a valid measure of A.

The study by Tarrow cited above provides an example of this logic. Tarrow's initial conclusion that the usual question "How interested are you in politics?" was providing an invalid measure of "political interest" among French farmers came from his observation that farmers, who appeared to have the lowest level of political interest in France on the basis of that question, had one of the highest levels of electoral participation. Because he could not conceive of high electoral participation occurring in the absence of high political interest, he concluded that the conventional measures, which had showed low political interest coinciding with high participation, must not have been measuring political interest.[4]

As another example of this kind of test, consider a measure of nations' hostility to each other, a measure based on content analysis of the nations' newspapers. If we found that two of the nations went to war against each other, yet the measure did not show an accompanying increase in feelings of hostility between the two, we would be suspicious of the validity of the measures.

Such an indirect test of validity is possible only when you are quite certain that β must go along with A. Otherwise, the absence of a relationship between β and α might mean *either* that α does not mirror A, *or* that β and A are not related. That kind of certainty is rare and may not be shared equally by every observer. This is a test which is not always, or even usually, possible; and it is one which is always rather subjective. But assessing the validity of measures is so important that an indirect test, when it can be used, greatly strengthens your findings.

---

[4] In this example, "political interest" corresponds to A, farmers' responses to the question on political interest corresponds to α, and farmers' electoral participation corresponds to β.

**THE IMPACT
OF RELIABILITY
AND VALIDITY**

It should be obvious that the only good measure is one which is both reliable and valid. Because social scientists often operate with measures which may be unreliable and/or invalid, however, it is worth considering what happens under those circumstances.

As it happens, unreliability and invalidity have rather different effects on the development of theory.

The effect of invalidity in a measure is simple and severe. If a measure is invalid, then there is no reason for us to expect any correspondence between the relationship we observe from the measures and the relationship we want to investigate.

The effect of unreliability (if the measures are valid) is more subtle. Unreliability will not impose a relationship at the measure level which is different in form from the relationship at the concept level. But to the extent that measures are unreliable, the relationship at the measure level will tend to be looser and weaker than the true relationship at the concept level. If the measures are sufficiently unreliable, the basic relationship can be so weakened that it will appear to us, from what we can observe, that there is no relationship at all.

This is illustrated in Table 4–1. The first two columns of the table give artificial figures for the closeness of elections in his district, and for his seniority, for each of ten congressmen. It is apparent from the figures in the first two columns that there is a relationship between the two, inasmuch as congressmen with safe districts tend to have greater seniority than those from marginal districts. The relationship is also quite strong, with

Table 4–1   Safe Districts Related to Seniority, Using Simulated Data

True Values		Less Reliable Measures		Very Unreliable Measures	
Seniority	Margin of Victory	Seniority	Margin of Victory	Seniority	Margin of Victory
32	18%	32.0	21.6%	12.8	9.0%
24	12	19.2	12.0	12.0	12.6
23	11	11.5	12.1	30.2	5.5
20	11	22.0	4.4	22.4	6.6
14	8	14.0	5.6	21.2	12.0
11	6	11.0	6.0	13.1	3.6
10	6	9.0	10.8	7.0	10.8
6	4	3.6	4.0	13.8	2.8
5	3	4.5	3.6	29.3	1.5
2	1	2.4	0.5	0.2	12.9

seniority increasing without exception as the congressmen's margins of victory increase.

In the third and fourth columns random error, such as might occur from clerical errors or other sources of unreliability, has been added to the basic figures. These new figures are less reliable measures than the original ones. In the fifth and sixth columns an even greater degree of random error has been added. Note that the basic relationship becomes weaker in the middle columns (there are more exceptions to the general tendency) and virtually disappears in the fifth and sixth columns. If we were to test the relationship between safe districts and seniority, and we had only the data from the last two columns in hand, we would conclude that there was no relationship.

In this chapter I have discussed problems in the accuracy of measurement. These problems turn out to be rather different depending on whether they stem from flux in the measure (the problem of reliability), or from a basic lack of correspondence between measure and concept (the problem of validity). In the next chapter, we shall look at another aspect of measurement, the question of how precisely a measure should be calibrated.

FURTHER DISCUSSION   A delightful book, which urges the use of varied measures to handle certain problems of validity, is *Unobtrusive Measures,* by Eugene J. Webb, Donald T. Campbell, Richard D. Schwartz, and Lee Sechrist (1966). The ideas presented in the book are both creative and sound, and the book itself is filled with interesting and highly unusual examples. Oskar Morgenstern gives a number of examples of problems in both the validity and reliability of measurement in economics, in *On the Accuracy of Economic Observations* (1950). "Errors," in the *International Encyclopedia of the Social Sciences* (1968), is valuable, particularly the essay by Frederick Mosteller in which he details a variety of possible sources of invalidity and unreliability.

PROBLEMS
OF
MEASUREMENT
PRECISION
5

The preceding chapter dealt with problems of the reliability and validity of measures. Those problems concerned the relationship between a measure and the concept which the measure is intended to mirror. In this chapter I shall discuss the "quality" of the measure itself—how precise it should be, how finely it must be calibrated, if it is to be useful.

In a recent book about Norwegian politics, Harry Eckstein felt that it was necessary to apologize for the fact that some measures he would use were subjective intangibles ("warmth in social relations," for instance, and "sense of community"), rather than precise numerical quantities.

> . . . many of the indicators used in the text may not be readily recognized as such by contemporary social scientists. By an indicator we usually mean nowadays a precisely ascertainable quantity that stands for some imprecise quantity (as GNP may indicate level of economic development, or as the number of casualties in revolutionary violence may indicate its intensity). I do use such quantities in what follows. More often, however, readily observable "qualities" are used as indicators of not-so-readily observable qualities. This strikes me as both defensible and desirable, for quantitative indicators are not always as "indicative" of what one wants to know as other observations, nor always obtainable. In overemphasizing quantities we sometimes miss the most telling data—in any case, data that may be reliable in their own right or used as checks on the inferences drawn from quantitative data. I conceive of all social behavior as a vast "data bank," only some of which is quantitatively aggregated in yearbooks and the like, and much of the rest of which may speak volumes to our purposes, if used circumspectly.[1]

[1] From Harry Eckstein, *Division and Cohesion in Democracy: A Study of Norway* (copyright © 1966 by Princeton University Press), footnote pp. 79–80. Reprinted by permission of Princeton University Press.

It is wrong that he should have felt the need to write this. This should have been an unnecessary justification, but unfortunately, precise measurement has become enough of a fetish in political science that it is no doubt always possible to find someone who will dismiss a piece of work because it is not "quantitative." In this chapter I hope to sort out just what kinds of precise quantification are helpful in political research.

The cardinal rule of measurement might read: *Use measurement which is as precise as possible, given the subject you are studying; do not waste information by imprecise measurement.* One theme of this chapter will be that this rule is as susceptible to violation by "quantifiers" as by "non-quantifiers." In order to discuss it further, I must first distinguish between two kinds of precision with which we shall be concerned. I shall call the first of these "precision in measures," and the second "precision in measurement."

PRECISION IN MEASURES   Precision in measures is what is generally referred to as "precision"—i.e., keeping the units of measurement relatively fine. For example, reporting a person's income in dollars is more precise than rounding it off to the nearest thousand dollars. Rounding income off to the nearest ten thousand dollars is still less precise—in fact, it is so imprecise that such a measure would be useless for most purposes. Similarly, reporting a person's religion as "Presbyterian," "reformed Jewish," "Greek Orthodox," and so on is more precise than reporting it as "Protestant," "Catholic," and "other."

Although as a general rule precision in measures is obviously a good thing, its importance can be overrated. First of all, how great a precision in measures we need is determined by what we wish to do with the data. If we were registering voters, for instance, any precision in measuring age that went beyond labeling people "under eighteen" and "over eighteen" would be unnecessary and possibly a nuisance as well.

In the usual sort of theory-oriented empirical research, however, we are not able to limit the necessary level of precision in this way. We usually are interested in looking at a variable generally and have no particular cutting point in mind.

Very frequently, however, even in theory-oriented research, too much precision in measures can be a nuisance. Consider Figure 5–1, which shows the relationship between age and participation in the 1968 presidential election. The figure is so chaotic that it is hard to tell what that relationship is.

Given the limited number of individuals (about two thousand) consulted in the poll, there is only a small number of respondents for each particular age. This means that the percent voting fluctuates a good deal from one age group to the next. (See the box, "Law of Large Numbers.")

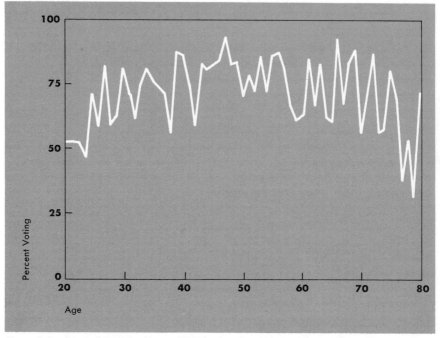

Figure 5–1   Age and Participation in 1968 Election: Age Measured by Years

Source: 1968 Presidential Election Survey, University of Michigan (Survey Research Center Study SRC–S523).

In the ensuing largely random fluctuation of percent voting, it is hard to pick out a systematic pattern in the relationship between age and participation in elections.

One way of handling this problem, of course, would be to expand the number of individuals studied. But this usually is not practical and may be impossible. If we study United States Presidents, for example, we are limited to thirty-seven cases.

Another way to handle the problem is to decrease the precision of the measure, creating a smaller number of categories with a larger number of cases in each.[2] This has been done in Figure 5–2, with age measured to the nearest half-decade, rather than to the nearest year. With the larger number of cases in each age class, the measures of percent voting fluctuate less and

[2] Reducing precision in this way to eliminate random noise in the data is appropriate only for chartmaking and visual presentation. Data analysis techniques such as regression analysis handle random noise in their own way. Reducing precision in measures may cause such techniques to give systematically inaccurate results. (See Chapter 7 for a description of regression analysis.)

Law of Large Numbers

The fact that the smaller the groups of individuals are, the more measures based on those groups will fluctuate, is one part of the Law of Large Numbers. (This law forms the basis for a great deal of statistics.) The fact is intuitively obvious. If one selected groups of one thousand people randomly and calculated the percent male, he would expect to get very nearly the national figure in all of them. With groups of one hundred, he would get increasingly erratic measurement. (It would not be unlikely for there to be 60 percent males in a hundred people, for example.) With groups of ten, there would be wild fluctuation; and with groups of one (the smallest possible "group") all groups would be either 0 or 100 percent male.

the form of the relationship between age and participation becomes clearer.

If it is true that sometimes we may be better off with less precision in our measures, then it appears that this sort of precision is not so important that research should be judged solely, or even largely, on how precise its

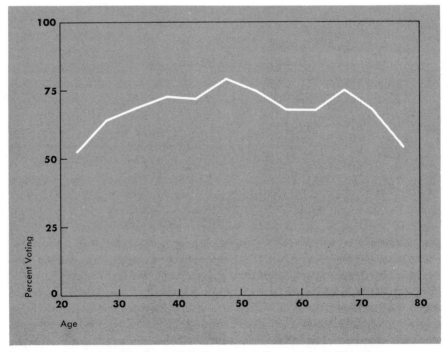

Figure 5–2   Age and Participation in 1968 Election: Age Measured by Half-Decades

measures are. On the other hand, although there are situations in which we may want to back off from precise measures, one should not conclude that precision is not helpful or important. To continue with the example of age and participation, if age were measured still less precisely than in Figure 5–2, we could lose some of the pattern which we saw there. If age were measured in units of thirty years, for example, we would find that 74.2 percent of those in the first unit (21–50) voted, and that 75.2 percent of those in the second unit (51–80) voted. From this we might conclude that age had little effect on participation!

The time to insure that your measures will be as precise as you want is when you are gathering data. There are various precautions that you can take. First of all, you can make sure that you include as large a number of cases as is practical, so that you will not have to reduce the precision farther than you would like.

In this connection, if you expect to be particularly concerned in your study with a specific group of the population, it makes sense to get an adequate number of the group into your study, even if that means ending up with data which are not "typical" of the whole population. This sort of selection is known as drawing a "stratified" sample.

For example, if you wanted to study the effects of different kinds of discrimination, you might draw up a sample consisting of equal numbers of WASPs, white ethnics, blacks, Puerto Ricans and Chicanos. Had you simply drawn a random sample of the population, you probably would have drawn too few Puerto Ricans and Chicanos, and you would have had to lump them together with either the blacks or the white ethnics.

Another precaution which you should take at the data-gathering stage is to make sure that you do not casually throw away precision which you might later regret having lost. When asking people their age, record the number of years old, not "under 30," "30–40," and the like. You can always group the data later if you want to; at this point you should save all the information you get. If you ask people their religion, write down "Presbyterian," "Roman Catholic," and so on—not "Protestant," "Catholic," and "Jew." Do not group the information you have until you have finished gathering it. You will have a better idea then of how fine a grouping you want to end up with.

If it is true, as the Cardinal Rule states, that it is important to be as precise as possible and not to waste information, these suggestions will help meet that rule. But the rule also states that we should be as precise as we can, *given the subject we are studying.* It is because of the limitations imposed by any topic of research that I have been careful not to overemphasize the importance of precision in measures in this section. Many questions in political science are such that the precision in measures is strictly limited. Eckstein's study, which he defended in the quotation given at the start of this chapter, is a case in point. He wanted to study the degree of "community" in Norway. This does not lend itself to finely calibrated measures.

It would be foolish to give up such studies just because of this. Precision in measures is important, but not indispensable. No one should stop studying the Presidency because the number of cases is limited; or stop studying past historical periods because data are limited and many kinds are "pregrouped" in inconvenient ways; or stop studying Soviet politics because many facts are hidden or grouped together.

PRECISION IN MEASUREMENT

The sort of precision discussed in the preceding section, "precision in measures," can be overemphasized. But the next sort, "precision in measurement," cannot. With "precision in measures" we attempted to preserve information by keeping distinctions as fine as was possible and practical. Another place at which we must work to preserve information is in the very process of measurement. There are qualitatively different ways to measure, some of which include whole kinds of information that are not included in others. The best ways are those that include the most kinds of information.

The most primitive way to measure a variable is simply to assign categories of it to the individuals being studied. This is often called *nominal* measurement. For example, to measure religion, we may label people "Catholic," "Protestant," "Jew," "other." To measure nationality we may label them "English," "German," "Russian," and so on. Nominal measurement places individuals into distinct categories of a variable, but it does not tell us anything about how the categories relate to each other.

If, in addition to assigning categories, we can rank the categories according to "how much" of the variable they embody, then we have achieved *ordinal* measurement. In such measurement, we have some idea of a scale which ideally might represent the variable, and the scores which we assign to individuals show whether they fall higher or lower than others on such a scale. Two examples are: social status, measured in some way such as "lower/working/middle/upper," and party identification, measured "strong Democrat/weak Democrat/independent/weak Republican/strong Republican."

Further precision in measurement is possible if, in addition to ranking the scores according to "how much" of the variable they represent, we can say how great the differences between the scores are. In order to do this, we must have some common unit with which to measure distance along the scale. Note that such a unit was lacking in the two examples of ordinal measurement. We could not say whether the difference in status between "working" and "middle" was greater than the difference between "lower" and "working." And we could not say whether the difference between "weak

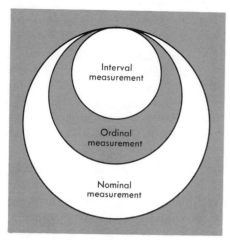

Figure 5–3 Levels of Precision

Republican" and "strong Republican" was greater than that between "independent" and "weak Republican."

If units exist with which we can measure the intervals between scores like these, then we have achieved *interval* measurement. Some examples of variables which are commonly measured intervally are: income (with the unit expressed in dollars), percent voting by districts (with the unit expressed in percentage points), governmental expenditure on a program (with the unit expressed either in dollars or in percentage points if measured as a percentage of the budget), air power (with the unit expressed in kilotons of bombing coverage, number of planes, or whatever), body counts (with the unit expressed in number of dead people), and so on.

It is clear that these levels of precision comprise a nesting progression, as shown in Figure 5–3. All interval measurements are also ordinal measurements and nominal measurements, and all ordinal measurements are also nominal measurements. That is, if we had an interval measure, but chose to ignore our knowledge of the distances involved between scores, we would still have scores on an ordinal measure. And if we had scores on an ordinal measure, but chose to ignore our knowledge of the relative ranking on the variable, we would still have a nominal measure, a set of distinct classes to which individuals were assigned.[3]

[3] A further refinement in precision is possible if, in addition to measuring the length of intervals along a scale, we can assign a score of zero to a point on the scale. We are then said to have "ratio" measurement (because we can then take one score as a multiple of another score, which is not possible if there is no zero point). I have not included ratio measurement in my discussion here because it has not, as yet, figured importantly in data analysis in the social sciences. All of the examples of interval scales which I have given are in fact also ratio scales. Generally, however, this is ignored and they are treated simply as interval scales.

To put it a little differently, if two individuals have different scores on a variable, then: (1) if the variable is measured nominally, we know that the two differ on the variable; (2) if the variable is measured ordinally, we know that the two differ on the variable *and* which one has the higher score; and (3) if the variable is measured intervally, we know that the two differ on the variable, which one has the higher score, *and* how much higher his score is than the other's.

The three major levels of measurement, then, are nominal, ordinal, and interval measurement. As a definition of "precision in measurement," we can say that measurement is relatively precise insofar as it operates at a level which is relatively informative. Accordingly, interval measurement is more precise than ordinal measurement, which is in turn more precise than nominal measurement.

THE SIN OF WASTING INFORMATION

Time and again data collected at a higher level of precision are collapsed down to a lower level, to simplify handling the data, writing reports, and so on. "Age" is often grouped into categories such as "young," "younger middle-aged," "older middle-aged," and "old"—an ordinal measure. Or income is grouped into "low," "middle," and "high."

Esthetically, however, it would seem better to know more about a subject, rather than less. This alone should be enough to justify the Cardinal Rule, as stated above: "Use measurements which are as precise as possible, given the subject you are studying; do not waste information by imprecise measurement." This esthetic consideration applies both to precision in measures and to precision in measurement. But inasmuch as I argued earlier that for practical purposes precision in measures sometimes should be sacrificed, it appears that the esthetic consideration is not compelling.

A more important reason for following the Cardinal Rule, one which applies only to precision in measurement, arises if we are interested in using the measures to study a relationship between two or more variables. In this case, we can do qualitatively different things with data measured at different levels of precision. Those things which are possible with more precise measurement are more varied than those which we can do with less precise measurement, and thus more valuable in developing theories. It is for this reason that precision in measurement is much more important than precision in measures. Let me provide an example at this point.

In Figure 5–4, the relationship between age and percent voting, which we looked at earlier, is presented in the form in which we might see it if (*a*) age were collapsed to a nominal measure and all knowledge of ranking and unit distance in it were lost; (*b*) age were collapsed to an ordinal mea-

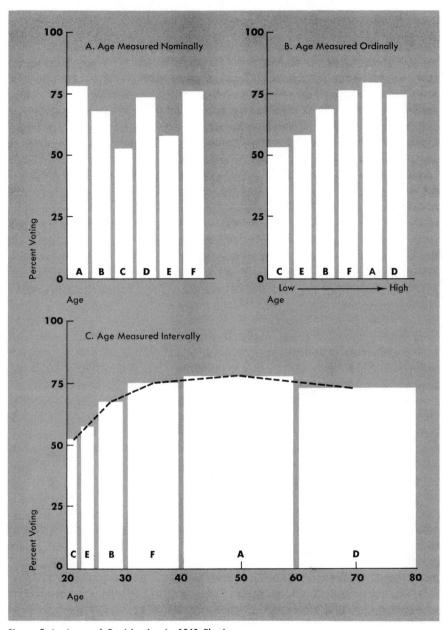

Figure 5–4 Age and Participation in 1968 Election

sure and the knowledge of unit distance in it were lost; and (c) age were maintained at an interval level of measurement.

In the first case, with age measured nominally, we can see that there is a relationship between age and participation in elections. This is indicated by the fact that different age groups participate at different rates. Only 54 percent of the individuals in category C vote, for instance, as compared with 80 percent of those in category A. If age and participation were not related, we would expect about the same percentage of individuals in each category to vote. With nominal measurement, this is all we can say—*that the variables are or are not related*.

In the second case, with ordinal measurement, we can say a good deal more. We now know the ranking of the different categories of age: C is youngest, E the next-to-youngest, and then come B, F, A, and D. In addition to seeing whether or not the variables are related, we can see *the pattern of the relationship*. In this case, that pattern is one of increasing participation with increasing age up to some point, and then a reversal, with participation decreasing as age continues up.

If age were measured intervally, we could say still more about the relationship. Interval measurement adds information about the magnitude of differences in age expressed by the categories. If age were measured intervally, we could see whether or not there was a relationship; we could see the pattern of the relationship; and we also could see *the rate at which one variable changed in response to changes in the other variable*.

In Figure 5–4, part *c*, the bars in the bar graph have been stretched to take into account added information that the categories represent the following age groups, measured in a common unit, years:

C	21–22
E	23–25
B	26–30
F	31–40
A	41–60
D	61–80

We can now see that the initial increase in participation, between the ages of twenty and thirty, is quite rapid; that participation peaks around fifty; and that there is then a more gradual decline. The dotted line tracing the path of the bars gives approximately the pattern which we had seen already in Figure 5–2. This suggests an interesting combination of processes: learning and acquiring the habit of voting during the first years of eligibility causes participation to rise rapidly at first; as this increase levels off, it is followed by a more gradual decline, perhaps due to enfeeblement. This is a richer description of the relationship than we could have gotten using the ordinal measurement.

Notice that in part *c* of Figure 5–4, greater precision in *measures* also would have been useful, especially a finer breakdown of ages above forty. With the greater precision in measures of Figure 5–2, we can see that what appears as a gradual decline after age fifty in part c is actually a much slower decline from about the mid-forties to age seventy, with a rapid decline in the seventies.

However, the information lost through the low precision in measures in part c is slight compared with the information lost by lowering the precision in measurement in parts a and b. Preserving a high level of precision in *measurement* deserves a strong priority in research.

ENRICHING THE LEVEL OF PRECISION IN MEASUREMENT

So far I have argued that we should try not to drop data carelessly to a lower level of measurement. By a similar argument, we should always try to *raise* data to a higher level of measurement, if it is possible to do so. As it turns out, this is an operation which frequently is possible, given a certain amount of boldness and ingenuity.

We can enrich our data in this way if we know something more about the data than is reflected in our measurement—in other words, if we have information about the data which would otherwise be wasted. This information may not be enough to provide neat, clean measurement at the higher level. If it were, we probably would have measured at the higher level in the first place. But generally, untidy measurement at a higher level is better than neat measurement at a lower level. A few examples may be the best way to show how measurement can be "enriched" in this way, by raising the level of measurement.

Some Examples of Enrichment   (A) You are studying the relationship between the colonial experience of new nations and the stability of democratic institutions in those nations. That is, you want to compare the stability of democratic institutions in former French colonies, former British colonies, former Dutch colonies, former United States colonies, and so on. One way to do this would be to simply treat the problem as one of a relationship involving nominal measurement.

But it is likely that you have in mind some underlying scale along which the colonial experience varied, depending on which country had done the colonizing, and that you are really interested in the relationship between this scale and the stability of democratic institutions. If you can array the different "mother countries" along this scale, then you can use them as an ordinal or interval measure of the scale.

You might, for example, be interested in whether or not the mother country tried to assimilate the native population to its own culture and the effect this had on the stability of the resulting institutions. On the scale "level of assimilation," the British colonial experience would rank low and the French quite high. The Dutch and American experiences would fall somewhere between these, with the United States possibly lower than the Dutch. For this particular purpose, then, the "mother countries" comprise at least an ordinal measure of the level of assimilation. If you could make a reasonably informed guess at the relative differences (e.g., Dutch rather close to the French; large gap between British and American), you even could bring it up to the level of rough interval measurement.

(B) You are studying the relationship between religion and political alienation. Religion could be treated as nominally measured (Jewish, old-Reformation Protestant, Roman Catholic, and so on). But as in example A, you may have an underlying dimension in mind, which causes you to expect a relationship between the two variables. You might be thinking in terms of the extent to which one's religion promotes an apocalyptic view of the universe. If so, then as in example A, you could take the different religions ranked by their apocalyptic content as an ordinal or interval measure of this scale. Jews would fall near the bottom of such a scale, and fundamental Protestants near the top.

Alternatively, your theory might be that religious groups, simply as social organizations, affect the level of alienation among their members. In this case you could array the different religions in terms of the size and "closeness" of their congregations, how democratic their legal structure is, or whatever.

Note that the "right" ordinal or interval arrangement of the nominal categories depends on which underlying scale you want to tap. The order of the religions will vary depending on the scale. Jews would fall low on the "apocalyptic" scale, for example, but high on the "closeness" scale.

You well might want to use a given nominal measurement twice or more in the same analysis, as a measure of different underlying scales. In example A, you might have been interested in predicting the stability of democratic institutions from two variables simultaneously: (1) the level of assimilation at which the "mother country" aimed, and (2) the extent of oppression and violence during the colonial period. The "mother countries" would be arrayed differently along these two scales, and each thus would represent a different mix of the two variables. The United States, for example, probably would fall above the middle in assimilation, but low in oppression; France, high in assimilation and toward the middle in oppression; Belgium low on assimilation but high on oppression; and so on.[4]

In working with ordinal variables (either "enriched" nominal variables

---

[4] Notice that the manner in which measurement of nominal variables has been enriched in these examples parallels the "dimensional analysis" which I urged in Chapter 4. Like vague, multi-dimensional concepts, nominal classifications involve an infinite number of dimensions. The various types of colonial experience cited above vary on degree of assimilation, extent of oppression, speed of economic development, geopolitical position, or what have you. Abstracting the appropriate ordered variable(s) from a nominally measured variable is much the same as abstracting the appropriate dimension(s) from a set of multi-dimensional concepts.

or variables which obviously are ordered from the outset) a common unit may appear immediately, and you can treat the variables readily and directly as interval measures. Abstracting the degree of "closeness" from religious affiliation, in example B, for instance, suggests one ready interval measure—average size of congregations—though this admittedly would be only a rough measure, whose validity would be questionable. But often, in order to enrich ordinal data, we must use a good deal of ingenuity, as in the next example.

(C) You want to measure the extent to which different educational programs tend to encourage pro-military or anti-military attitudes. You can distinguish three types of educational programs: military academy; general university, with participation in ROTC; general university, without participation in ROTC. These form an ordinal measure of "militariness" readily enough, with the military academy highest and the non-ROTC program lowest. Can you make an interval measure out of this ranking?

Fortunately, you have some additional information on the subject. In a study of Annapolis midshipmen, ROTC, and non-ROTC students, it was found that 39 percent of the midshipmen thought the American military budget was too small; 10 percent of the ROTC students agreed, as did 4 percent of the non-ROTC students.[5] If you are willing to assume that the Naval Academy is typical of the military academies and that there is a linear relationship between the pro-military orientation of an educational program and the percentage of its students who believe that the military budget is too small, then this information allows you to reconstruct the interval measure implicit in the ordered variable. (See the box, "Linear Relationship.")

If the degree of pro-military orientation in ROTC programs increases support of higher budgets by six percentage points over non-ROTC students, but the Naval Academy increases budget support by twenty-nine percentage points over ROTC students, then (given your assumptions) the interval between military academies and ROTC must be 4.83 times as great as the interval between ROTC and non-ROTC. This is demonstrated geometrically in Figure 5–5.

Here I have drawn two of the many possible linear relationships between the "military content" of education and support for the defense budget. It should be clear that the same principle would hold for any linear relationship. Because you know the scores on budget support for non-ROTC, ROTC, and the Naval Academy, you can look across the graph to see where they should fall on the line showing the relationship. Non-ROTC falls at A, ROTC at B, and the Naval Academy at C. Now, look down the graph to see what scores on "military content" must be associated with positions A, B, and C on the line. These scores are A', B', and C'. Of course, you do not have units in advance in which to measure military content, but it is appar-

[5] Peter Karsten *et al.*, 1971.

Linear Relationship

A relationship between two variables is *linear* if one variable changes by a constant amount with a change of one unit in the second variable, regardless of the value of the second variable. The relationship in graph A is linear; y increases by one-half unit when x changes by one unit, no matter what value x started with. The relationship in Graph B is nonlinear. Here, if x is high, a unit change in x produces relatively little change in y; if x is low, a unit change in x produces relatively great change in y.

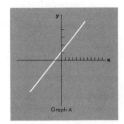

Thus, the relationship in graph A can be expressed by a straight line, inasmuch as the relationship is the same at all values of x. The relationship in Graph B must be expressed by a curve which tilts differently at different values of x, inasmuch as the relationship between the two variables is different for different values of x.

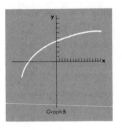

ent that whatever units you conceive of, and whatever linear relationship between the two variables exists, the distance from B′ to C′ must be approximately five times the distance from A′ to B′. (To be exact, the ratio of the distances is 4.83.)

This gives you all you need to construct an interval measure—that is, an estimate of the relative differences (intervals) between scores of the measure. Because an interval measure does not assume that a zero point is known, you can arbitrarily pick the unit in which to express your measure. You might assign 1.0 to non-ROTC, and 2.0 to ROTC, in which case military academy would have to be 6.83. You might assign 4.0 to non-ROTC and 8.0 to the academy; ROTC would then have to be 27.32. Most simply, the scores might be assigned: non-ROTC, 4; ROTC, 10; and academy, 39.

(D) In the example above, a rather precise piece of outside information was used to tell how long the intervals should be. Often you do not have a precise guide such as this; but you still may know somewhat more than nothing about the length of the intervals. Consider a problem in which you want to measure the national power of Costa Rica, Spain, Great Britain, and the Soviet Union.[6] The *order* is clear, and a timid researcher would be

---

[6] Although I am using "national power" as an example here, for most purposes this would be broken down more profitably into component dimensions, such as "diplomatic influence," "economic power," and "military power."

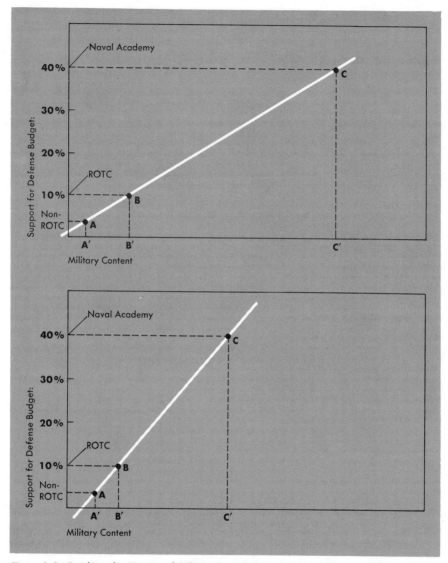

Figure 5–5   Enriching the Measure of Military Content

content to treat this as an ordinal variable. On the other hand, you know that the intervals are not equal, and you know which intervals are greater than others. You could create a quite acceptable, though rough, interval measure of the national power of the various countries simply by assigning arbitrary interval lengths in accordance with your general idea of the magnitudes involved. You might choose, for example: Costa Rica, 1; Spain, 4; Great Britain, 20; and the Soviet Union, 60. The measure is rough and subjective, but it could be refined by bringing to bear the impressions of other knowledgeable observers with regard to relative national power. Most importantly, measuring in this way does not ignore the valuable collection of outside information—most of it admittedly undigested—which you already possess.

The interval measures which you would get in examples C and D might not leave you fully satisfied. Because of the indirect chain of reasoning in example C, and the assumptions required for it, and because of the arbitrary decisions to be made in example D, there is plenty of room for errors to occur. The question remains: are you better off with such rough interval measures, or are you better off ignoring the size of intervals and treating the variables as ordinal measures? Given the wider range of theoretical concerns one can cover using interval data, I think the answer is obvious. It makes sense to use all the information we have about a question, even if we must supplement that information with assumptions and hunches. The alternative is to ignore a portion of what we know. Taking the "safer" course allows us to measure at a level at which we can be relatively confident, but it allows us to say relatively less interesting things about the variable we are measuring.

Enriching measurement in this way is a research technique for which the researcher's creativity and ingenuity are critical. One mark of a good researcher should be that he boldly seeks out all chances—not just the obvious ones, not just the safe ones—to raise the level of measurement in his work.

QUANTIFIERS AND NONQUANTIFIERS AGAIN

This discussion of precision in measures and precision in measurement has centered on the work of "quantifiers" (those who work by preference with objective data, and especially with numerical data), for it was more convenient to present it in that way. But the same general conclusions hold for "nonquantifiers" as well.[7] To return to the quotation from Eckstein with which I introduced this chapter, it is clear that he is interested in doing the same things as "quantifiers" do, but in a different way. He wants to measure variables and to assess relationships between those variables. His subject matter, however, rarely allows him to use objective or numerical measures.

[7] Let me repeat my earlier admonition. Being a "quantifier" or "nonquantifier" is not an either/or question. The extent to which a researcher uses objective data is generally not a matter of his personality, but rather of the subject he is studying and the data available for that subject.

For many variables in which he is interested, he can use only vague descriptions, such as "rather strong sense of community," "highly developed team spirit," and so on. Most of these descriptions must depend on his subjective judgment, rather than on impersonal outside indicators.

Can this sort of work be described in terms of precision in measures and precision in measurement? Do the rules I have prescribed in this chapter hold for this sort of work, as they do for more quantitative work? First of all, we may note that measuring variables in this way simply exercises the same sort of boldness that I urged in enriching data to a higher level of measurement. More importantly, we can see that this is primarily a problem of precision in measures, not of precision in measurement. A nonquantifier can measure things only approximately, but there is no particular reason why he cannot try to approximate interval measurement rather than nominal measurement.

For example, a student of Soviet politics might suggest that the higher a Soviet politician rises in the hierarchy, the less likely he is to press for the interests of particular groups. This statement approximates a relationship between two variables measured at the ordinal level ("height in the hierarchy" and "likelihood of pressing"). Working more boldly and imaginatively, he might approximate interval measurement. He might state, for example, that the higher a Soviet politician rises in the hierarchy, the less likely he is to press for the interest of particular groups; that this shift occurs very sharply as he moves from some particular level of the hierarchy to another; that the shift continues from there on up the hierarchy at a diminished rate; and that finally, near the top of the hierarchy, the process reverses itself, with the men at the top feeling secure enough to concern themselves more than those immediately below them with the interests of particular groups.[8] This is certainly a richer statement than the earlier version, but it is no more "quantified" than the other. It is still based on subjective descriptions, made in the absence of objective indicators. The only difference is that in the second case the researcher enriches the level of measurement at which he is working.

FURTHER DISCUSSION

A readable presentation along the lines developed in this chapter is Edward R. Tufte, 1968-69.

Two questions which you might consider are:

1. Why would the technique in example C not be appropriate if the relationship between "military content" and "support for defense budget" were nonlinear? What might you do in this case?

2. "Ratio" measurement is interval measurement for which, in addition to being able to measure the difference between different values of the measure, it is

---

[8] I have no idea whether this is a reasonable theory. It is purely hypothetical.

possible to assign the value zero to some point on the measure. (See footnote 3 above.) One difference between interval and ratio measurement is that, whereas it is possible to add and subtract interval measures, it is possible to add and subtract, *multiply,* and *divide* ratio measures. It is possible to say that a given score is twice as great as another score, given ratio measurements; this is not possible with simple interval measurement. Fahrenheit temperature is an example of an interval measure that is *not* a true ratio measure, even though "zero" is arbitrarily assigned to one point on the scale. It is not true, for example, that a temperature $+20°F.$ is half as "hot" as $+40°F.$ In this chapter, I pointed out that the different levels of measurement were important because it was possible to make a greater variety of statements about relationships between variables which were measured in "advanced" ways. What statements might be made about relationships between ratio-measured variables that could not be made about relationships between interval-measured variables?

CAUSAL THINKING, AND THE DESIGN OF RESEARCH

6

So far, everything we have looked at in this book has been justified in terms of how useful it is in establishing relationships between variables. It is time now to look more closely at what a "relationship" is, and how we interpret it.

Two variables are related if certain values of one variable tend to coincide with certain values of the other variable. Thus, social class and party vote are related in the United States, because those who vote Republican tend to be from the middle and upper classes. We have seen many such examples of relationships in earlier chapters.

If, in addition, we consider that the values of one variable *produce* the values of the other variable, then the relationship is a *causal relationship*. The example of class and voting is an example of a causal relationship. We feel that there is something about the social class of which one is a member that makes him more likely to vote in a certain way. Therefore, we say that social class is a "cause" of the party vote. It is not merely true that the two variables tend to coincide; they tend to coincide *because values of the one tend to produce distinct values of the other.*

Empirical, theory-oriented political research is almost exclusively concerned with *causal* relationships. As I pointed out earlier, a theory in its simplest form usually consists of three things—independent variables (which we think of as doing the "producing"), dependent variables (which we think of as being "produced"), and causal statements linking the two.[1]

In this chapter, I shall first discuss the idea of "causation." I shall follow this by a discussion of research design. Research design—the way in which we structure the gathering of data—strongly affects the nature of the causal interpretation we can put on the results of research. These two topics, research design and the nature of causation, which might seem unrelated, are in fact closely linked.

[1] See above, page 14.

THE SUBJECTIVE NATURE OF CAUSATION

The most important thing to note about causal thinking is that it is quite subjective. In this regard, the assertion of a *causal relationship* differs from the mere assertion of a *relationship,* which is a rather objective statement. In the example of social class and the vote, for instance, there is objective evidence for the existence of a relationship. But a causal interpretation of this relationship is much more subjective. It might be argued, for instance, that class does not produce the vote, but that both are produced by something else—the ethnic, religious, and racial conflicts which have surfaced often in American politics. Thus, someone could argue—and it would not be an unreasonable argument—that class is not a cause of the vote. Rather, he might say, certain ethnic groups tend to vote for the Democrats, and these same groups, simply by accident, also tend to be working-class. Therefore, the coincidence of class and party votes is just that—a coincidence. Distinguishing between his version of the relationship and the more common version is in large part a matter of judgment.

Almost every situation in which we wish to make causal statements is similar to this example. The question of whether or not there is a relationship is objectively testable. The question of whether the relationship is a causal one, and of which variable causes which, is largely a subjective one. Generally speaking, all that we know directly from our data is that two variables tend to occur together. To read causality into such co-occurence, we must add something more.

Consider two further examples: If we see that people who smoke regularly have a greater incidence of heart disease than nonsmokers, we might conclude that smoking causes heart disease. If we see that those senators who conform to the informal rules of the Senate tend to be the ones whose bills get passed, we might conclude that conformity is rewarded in the Senate.

In both cases, we observe that two phenomena tend to occur together (smoking and heart disease, conformity and success). Our interpretation of this is that one of the phenomena causes the other. This interpretation is a subjective one.

As we saw in the class/vote example, it is *not* true that we always make a causal interpretation whenever two phenomena tend to coincide. The notion of cause involves more than that. Winter does not cause Spring, though the one follows the other regularly. Similarly, hair color does not cause political party preference, though it is probably true in the United States that blonds, who are relatively likely to be white and Protestant, are more apt to be Republicans than Democrats. To qualify as a "causal" relationship, the coincidence of two phenomena must include the idea that one of them *produces* the other.

ELIMINATING ALTERNATIVE CAUSAL INTERPRETATIONS

A causal interpretation is something that cannot come solely from our observations. But by setting up a study in certain ways, and by manipulating the data appropriately, we can settle *some* of the problems in making causal interpretations. In the above example of hair color, for instance, we might have looked only at WASPs, and compared blonds and brunettes. If we then found that blond WASPs did not tend to be more Republican than brunette WASPs, we could infer that hair color did not cause party preference.

In general, where we think that a third variable is causing two other variables to coincide accidentally, as in this hair color example, we can tell from our data whether the apparently causal relationship is false. By "holding constant" the third variable, we can see whether it has caused the original two variables to coincide, in such a way as to make it appear that one caused the other. In the hair color example, we artificially held social position constant by looking only at WASPs. Thus there were no differences in social position among the individuals studied. If blonds and brunettes no longer differed in their politics when this was done, then we were able to infer that the original difference between the blonds and the brunettes was due to the fact that the former were relatively more likely to be WASPs. We then could conclude that hair color did not cause political preference.[2]

Thus, there are techniques by which we can manipulate our data to eliminate *some* of the alternative causal interpretations of a relationship. But there is always one question about causation which in field research is purely subjective, and which no techniques of data handling can resolve completely. Given that two variables are causally related, this is the question: which of the variables causes which?

Suppose that two phenomena coincide, and that you think there is a causal relationship between them. The question of which is the cause and which the result requires you to make a subjective judgment. One useful convention in Western culture—but it is only a convention—is that causation works forward in time. Adherence to this convention frequently simplifies the question of which of two variables functions as a cause of the other. If we can establish that one of the variables precedes the other, then, if we are sure that there is causation between the two, it is clear which variable must be the cause. For example, we assume that pulling a trigger causes the shot that follows that action, rather than vice versa.

Although this convention frequently simplifies things for us, there are many research problems in which we cannot use it. Survey research, in

---

[2] For a more complete discussion of "holding constant," see below, pages 98–101.

Table 6–1   Economic Status, Religion, and Party Preference

	Below Average Status			Above Average Status	
	Catholic	Non-Catholic		Catholic	Non-Catholic
Democrat	100	10	Democrat	10	0
Republican	0	10	Republican	10	100

which variables usually are measured just once and in a single interview, is a case in point. If voters who like the Republican Party also tend to oppose welfare programs, which causes which?

As another example, consider the fact that many important social variables are with a person from childhood, so that one can never be said to precede another in his life. Race, religion, social class, and other factors are intermingled; how can we sort out causal relationships involving them? The controversy over whether blacks' low performance on achievement tests is due to their innate ability as a race or to their experiences in growing up, which are inextricably involved with their race, is a case in point.[3] Table 6–1, which relates hypothetical data on economic status, religion, and party preference, furnishes another example of the same problem. In Table 6–1, we are faced with three variables which are all closely related with one another: economic status, religion, and party preference. The problem is to sort out the directions of causation among these variables. That is, we know that all three tend to *vary together:* low economic status, being a Catholic, and preferring the Democrats tend to coincide; as do high economic status, not being a Catholic, and preferring the Republicans. But which of the variables *produce* which?

Presumably, party choice does not cause either economic status or religion (although it might be argued, for instance, that in the days of the "Solid South," choosing to be a Republican could have resulted in economic loss for a Southerner). But practically all of the Catholics in this table are of "below average" status, and vice versa. How can we tell from the table whether religion causes party choice (and the relationship between eco-

---

[3] I am assuming, for the purposes of this example, that such tests are valid measures with which to compare people's innate abilities. This is a whole separate question, which has not been resolved.

nomic status and party choice is mere coincidence), or whether economic status causes party choice (and the relationship between religion and party choice is mere coincidence), or whether both function as causes of party choice?

The answer, of course, is that we cannot tell this from the table. Our judgment must be subjective, and the choice is a difficult one. In particular, the convention that causation must flow forward in time cannot help us sort out the causal priorities in this case, inasmuch as both religion and economic status are with a person largely from childhood.

SUMMARY

Let me pull together the argument to this point. It generally is not enough for us to note that two phenomena coincide. We generally want to interpret also *why* they coincide. There are three interpretations available to us, and our choice from among them is primarily subjective:

I. Causation is Not Involved at All   The phenomena coincide because they logically must coincide. That is, their coincidence is tautologically determined. The example above of the succeeding seasons was of this type. Spring follows Winter by definition; therefore, we do not think of Winter as producing Spring. A common example of this situation in the social sciences occurs when two slightly different measures of the same thing coincide. We would expect them to coincide, simply because they measure the same thing; we do not think of either of them as causing the other. For example, the votes of congressmen on educational spending tend to coincide with their votes on welfare spending. This is not because their votes on one issue cause them to vote the way they do on the other. Rather, both votes are an expression of their general disposition to spend money on social programs. We must decide from outside the data at hand whether a coincidence of two phenomena is of this type or involves causation.

II. Causation is Involved Somewhere   This may mean one of two things. Either: (A) *The coincidence we observe is a result of outside factors which cause the two phenomena at hand, and thus neither of these phenomena causes the other.* The example of hair color and party preference was of this sort. By setting up the study appropriately, we can control for various outside factors in order to see whether this is what is going on. In the hair color example, such a control was used. To this extent, we can see *from the data* whether the coincidence of the phenomena is of this sort. But we are still not exempt from making assumptions, for we must first have assumed the outside factor(s) causally prior to the two coincident phenomena. As I pointed out in the example of religion, economic status, and voting, this is not always an easy decision to make. If it is possible to set up a true experiment (described in the next section), then we can eliminate the possibility of situation II–A. But this is rare in "field" social sciences such as political science or sociology.

Or: (B) *One of the phenomena causes the other.* Here we have, finally, a causal statement. We are still not finished making assumptions, of course, for we still must decide which of the phenomena is the cause and which the effect. That is a subjective decision, though often we are aided in making it by the convention that causation must run forward in time.

As I have said so often in this book, one of the pleasures of research is that nothing in it is automatic. Even the most "quantitative" techniques do not take away our obligation (and our right) to be creative and imaginative. The fact that causal analysis is ultimately subjective may trouble us—objectivity always seems more comforting than the responsibility imposed by subjective judgment—but in a way it is also a great comfort, inasmuch as it keeps us, and what we do with our minds, at the heart of our research.

A FEW BASICS OF RESEARCH DESIGN It should be evident from the discussion so far that the basic problem in causal analysis is that of eliminating alternative causal interpretations. Whenever two variables vary together (are related, coincide), there is a variety of causal sequences which might account for their doing so. A might cause B, B might cause A, both A and B might be caused by something else, or there might be no causation involved. Our task is to eliminate all but one of these, thus leaving an observed relationship, together with a single causal interpretation of it. Some of these alternatives can be eliminated only if we make assumptions from outside the actual study. But we also can design the study itself in such a way that certain alternatives are impossible. This will leave an interpretation which is dependent on fewer subjective assumptions and will thus make us more certain of the results.

Consider these examples:

1. Agency Study An organizational analysis is made of a government agency, in which each worker keeps track of his output for a week. The organization is then restructured so as to decentralize decision making. After the reform, another week's tabulation shows increased output. Conclusion: decentralized decision making increases output.

2. The Spock Revolution During the 1950s, American child-rearing practices became more "permissive." In the 1960s,

American youth became more radical. Conclusion: permissive child-rearing produces radical youth.

3. *Organizing the Poor*   In anticipation of a major campaign to organize the poor of a city, a survey is taken among them to measure their interest in politics. At the end of the organizing campaign, the same people are asked the same questions a second time. It turns out that those who were contacted by the campaign workers have indeed acquired an increased interest in politics, compared with those who were not. Conclusion: the campaign has increased the political awareness of the poor.

4. *Tax-reform Mail*   The *Congressional Quarterly* reports the proportion of each senator's mail which favored tax reform. Comparing these figures with the senators' votes on a tax-reform bill, we see that those senators who had received relatively favorable mail tended to vote for the bill, whereas those who had received relatively unfavorable mail tended to vote against it. Conclusion: how favorable a senator's mail was on tax reform affected whether or not he voted for it.

5. *Presidential Lobbying*   In an attempt to measure his influence over Congress, the President randomly selects half the members of the House. He conducts a straw vote to find out how all the members of the House intend to vote on a bill important to him. He then lobbies intensively among the half he has randomly selected. In the final vote in the House, the group that he had lobbied shifted in his favor, compared with what he could have expected from the earlier straw vote; the other half voted about as predicted from the straw vote. Conclusion: his lobbying had helped the bill.

Let us look at the design of these studies, to see how many alternative causal interpretations each can eliminate.

DESIGNS WITHOUT A CONTROL GROUP

In the first two examples, the design is of the form: (1) measure the dependent variable; (2) observe that the independent variable occurs; (3) measure the dependent variable again; (4) if the dependent variable has changed, ascribe that to the occurence of the independent variable. Thus, in "Agency Study," (1) the workers' output is tabulated; (2) the organizational structure is decentralized; (3) the workers' output is once again tabulated; and (4) the conclusion is reached. This kind of design operates *without a control group*. As a result, there are a number of alternative causal sequences which might produce the same result.

For example, a plausible alternative explanation for the increased productivity might be that the initial measurement of production, in which each worker kept track of his output for a week, focused the workers' attention on productivity in a way that had not been done before, leading them to improve their productivity. In other words, it was not the decentralization of the agency, but the study itself, which caused productivity to rise.[4]

Had the study included a second agency as a control, in which output was measured at the same times as in the first agency, but in which there was no decentralization, the alternative explanation would not have been plausible. That is, if the increased productivity in "Agency Study" had been due simply to the act of measuring, then productivity in the control agency (in which the same measurements were taken as in the first agency) also should have increased. Accordingly, if we found that productivity increased more in the reorganized agency than in the control agency, we would know that this could not have been because of the act of measuring, for both agencies had undergone the same measurements. That particular alternative interpretation would have been eliminated by the design of the study. In conducting the study without a control, the alternative interpretation can be eliminated only by assuming it away, which seems very risky.

"The Spock Revolution" provides an example of another sort of alternative explanation which may be plausible if the research design does not include a control group. It is quite possible that other things which occurred between the two "measurements" of youth's radicalism (roughly, the early fifties and the late sixties) were the cause of the increased radicalism among young people, rather than the changed patterns of child-rearing. The change in educational policies after Sputnik, the Civil Rights movement in the South, the Vietnam War, increased affluence—all might be proposed as alternative causes. If it were possible to construct a control group of American youths whose parents had not changed their child-rearing practices, then these alternative explanations could be tested and perhaps eliminated. The control group would have experienced all the alternative causes in the same way as the original group. If it did not become as radical as the original, the alternative explanations of the shift would not be plausible.

The same general alternative explanation also might have applied to

---

[4] A famous example of this sort is the "Hawthorne" study, in which an attempt was made to measure how much productivity increased when factories were made brighter and more pleasant. As it turned out, the groups of workers who were placed in better surroundings did show major increases in productivity. But so did control groups, whose surroundings had not been improved. The novelty of taking part in an experiment, the attention paid to the workers, and increased social cohesiveness among the groups which had been set apart for the purposes of the experiment—all these raised productivity irrespective of the experimental changes in physical working conditions which were made for some (but not all) of the groups. See Roethlisberger and Dickson, 1939.

"Agency Study." If something else had happened between the two measurements of productivity—the weather improved, Christmas came, the President urged greater productivity, or whatever—this might have been the true cause of the increased production. Again, using a second agency as a control could eliminate such alternative explanations.

"The Spock Revolution," incidentally, is an example of how difficult it may be to include a control group in a design. Where an event affects the entire population you wish to study, it may be impossible to build a control group. For example, the existence of the United Nations has affected the foreign policy of every country in the world since 1945. How can a student of international politics distinguish its effect on countries' foreign policy from the effects of the Soviet-American rivalry, the development of atomic weapons, the liberation of former colonies, and so on—all of which have happened at the same time? He cannot, of course. It is simply not possible to provide a control group of countries for whom the United Nations has not existed.

USE OF A CONTROL GROUP

The "Natural Experiment"   "Organizing the Poor" is an example of a design in which a control group has been added to handle the sorts of problems suggested above. It is a "natural experiment," a design in which a test group (that is, a group exposed to the independent variable) and a control group (a group *not* exposed to the independent variable) are used, but in which the investigator has no control over who falls into the test group and who falls into the control group. In "Organizing the Poor," the matter of who was contacted by the campaign workers was decided by the workers' own choice of whom to contact and by the extent to which different people made themselves available for contact by the campaign workers. The "natural experiment" design is of the form: (1) measure the dependent variable for a population before they are exposed to the independent variable; (2) wait until some of them have been exposed to the independent variable; (3) measure the dependent variable again; (4) if between measurings the group which was exposed (called the "test group") has changed relative to the control group, ascribe this to the effect of the independent variable on the dependent variable. Thus, in "Organizing the Poor," (1) a number of poor people were surveyed as to their interest in politics; (2) the campaign occurred; (3) the same poor people were surveyed again; (4) those who had been contacted by the campaign were compared with those who had not. This design eliminates most of the alternative explanations which cropped up in working without a control group.

However, the "natural experiment" still allows alternative explanations, which we must face. Because the researcher does not have control over who is exposed to the independent variable, it may be that the group which is exposed is one which has a different predisposition to change than the control group. In "Organizing the Poor," for instance, the campaign workers are likely to have approached those poor whom they could most easily get interested in politics. Also, those among the poor who were most resistant to change might not have let the campaign workers in the door or might have been chronically absent when the campaign workers tried to contact them. Accordingly, a plausible alternative explanation in "Organizing the Poor" is that the poor who were contacted by the campaign increased their interest in politics more than those who were not contacted *simply because they were the ones who were becoming more interested in politics at that time, regardless of the campaign.* This alternative must be either assumed away or controlled by using a design in which the researcher can determine who falls into the test group and who falls into the control group. A design which accomplishes this is a "true experiment," but before going on to discuss this, let me discuss a poor cousin of the natural experiment.

The Natural Experiment without Premeasurement

This is a design in which no measurements are made before subjects are exposed to the independent variable. This design follows the form: (1) measure the dependent variable for subjects, some of whom have been exposed to the independent variable (the test group) and some of whom have not (the control group); (2) if the dependent variable differs between the groups, then ascribe this difference to the effect of the independent variable.

The "Tax-reform mail" example is of this sort. In "Tax-reform mail," (1) senators' votes on a tax reform bill were noted, and (2) the votes of senators who had received favorable mail were compared with the votes of those who had not. The same kind of alternative explanation which has to be dealt with in natural experiments has to be dealt with in this design also. As in "Organizing the Poor," it may be that heavier pro-tax-reform mail went to senators who already were moving into a tax-reform position even without the mail. Such senators, about whom there might have been a great deal of speculation in the press, could have attracted more mail than did other senators.

Moreover, this design permits additional alternative explanations, beyond those which apply to the natural experiment. In the tax-reform example, it is probable that people were more likely to write letters favoring reform to senators they thought would agree with them. This is usually true of mail to congressmen and senators. In other words, the relationship between a senator's vote on the bill and the mail he received might be due not to effect the mail has on his vote, but to the fact that senators who were already pro-reform got more pro-mail and those who were already anti-reform got more anti. This alternative could not apply to a natural experiment. In the natural experiment, it would have been clear from the initial measurement whether or not those who fell into the test group had initially been different from those falling into the control group. In fact, what is compared in the natural experiment is not the measured variables themselves, but how the two groups change between measurements.

To sum up, the natural experiment without premeasurement is a design in which the test group and the control group are compared with respect to a dependent variable only after they have been exposed to the independent variable. It involves the same sorts of alternative explanations as the natural experiment does, plus some others which result from the fact that the investigator does not know what the test group and the control group looked like before the whole thing started.

THE TRUE EXPERIMENT

In neither of the two versions of the "natural" experiment above did the investigator have any control over who fell into the test group and who fell into the control group. If the investigator does have such control, he can perform a *true experiment*. In a true experiment, (1) some subjects are *assigned* to the test group and some to the control group; (2) the dependent variable is measured for both groups; (3) then the independent variable is administered to the test group; and (4) the dependent variable is measured again for both groups; (5) if the test group has changed between the first and second measurements in a way that is different from the control group, this difference is ascribed to the presence of the independent variable.

Because the investigator can control who falls into which group, he can set the groups up in such a way that they are equivalent. (The best, and simplest, way to do this is to assign subjects randomly to one group or the other.) The advantage of making the groups equivalent is that he can thereby eliminate many of the alternative causal interpretations which had to be assumed away in the various natural experiment designs. If the groups are equivalent to start with, for example, a difference in how the groups change cannot be due to the fact that the individuals in the test group were more prone to change in certain ways than those in the control group. Thus, the problem which the investigators faced in "Organizing the Poor" is eliminated.

"Presidential lobbying" is an example of the true experiment. Here, (1) the President chose half of the House randomly to be the test group, leaving the other half as the control; (2) he took a straw vote to measure the dependent variable (vote) for both groups; (3) he lobbied the test group; (4) the bill was voted on; and (5) he compared the voting of the two groups in order to see whether his lobbying had made a difference. Working with this design, the President would be pretty certain that a disproportionately favorable change among those he lobbied was due to his efforts. If he had not been able to control who was lobbied, he would have been faced with plausible alternative causal interpretations.

A COMPARISON OF THE DESIGNS

Table 6–2 summarizes the various research designs discussed in this chapter and some of the alternative explanations applicable to them. In presenting the designs graphically, an asterisk (*) indicates that a group has been exposed to a stimulus or is distinguished in some other way so as to constitute a "test group"; M indicates that the dependent variable has been measured for the group; and R (used to describe the "true experiment") indicates that individuals have been assigned randomly to the groups.[5]

RESEARCH DESIGNS IN POLITICAL RESEARCH

The natural experiment without premeasurement is the most commonly used single design in political research. A few examples will indicate the broad use of the design: (1) any voting study which shows that persons of a certain type (working-class, educated, male, or what have you—the test group) vote differently than those who are not of this type (the control group); (2) any study of officials which shows that those who work under certain conditions (test group) perform differently than those who do not (control group)—for instance, a study by Samuel Eldersveld, in which he found that party workers were more effective in precincts which were not "safe" districts for the opposition party; [6] (3) most "policy output" studies, such as one by Fry and Winters, which showed that states with high participation in elections (test group) tended to have governmental policies which were more helpful to the poor than states with low participation in elections (control group).[7]

In short, any research is an example of the natural experiment without premeasurement if it: (1) takes two or more types of subjects and compares their values on a dependent variable; and (2) infers that the difference on the dependent variable is the result of their difference on whatever it is that

---

[5] This notation has been adapted from Campbell and Stanley, 1963.
[6] Eldersveld, 1964, p. 424.
[7] Fry and Winters, 1970; for the particular finding I refer to here, see the table on p. 520.

Table 6–2   Selected Research Designs

Type	Graphic Presentation	Example from this Chapter	Selected Alternative Causal Interpretations
Observation with no control group	Test group: M * M	"Agency Study" "Spock Revolution"	The first measurement itself may have caused the change observed in the second measurement; or something else which happened at the same time as * may have caused the change.
Natural experiment without pre-measurement	Test group: * M Control group: M	"Tax-reform mail"	Those who made their way into the test group may have been more likely to change than those who made their way into the control group; or those who made their way into the test group may have been different from those in the control group even before they experienced *.
Natural experiment	Test group: M * M Control group: M M	"Organizing the poor"	Those who made their way into the test group may have been more likely to change than those who made their way into the control group.
True experiment	Test group: R M * M Control group: R M M	"Presidential lobbying"	None of the alternatives which I have discussed in this chapter apply. This design permits only a very few alternative explanations. Consult the source cited at the end of this chapter.

Source: This notation has been adapted from Donald T. Campbell and Julian C. Stanley, Experimental and Quasi-Experimental Designs for Research (Chicago: Rand McNally Co., 1963).

distinguishes them as "types." [8] This really describes the bulk of political research.

As we saw in the earlier sections, this design is far from satisfactory.

[8] It is apparent here and in the examples which preceded this that I am taking some liberty with the notion of "control group." Where, say, rates of participation in the middle class and working class are compared, it is not at all clear which class is the "test" group and which is the "control." The distinction is even muddier when one compares several groups simultaneously, such as voters from several age groups. But the logic of what is done here is the same as in the strict test/control situation, where the dependent variable is compared among groups of subjects distinguished by their values on the independent variable. I find it convenient and revealing to treat this sort of analysis in terms of the analogy to experiments.

It permits relatively many alternative causal interpretations, which are difficult to handle. Nevertheless, this design remains the most popular one in political science. Designs which operate without a control group require us to assume away even more difficult alternative causal interpretations than those suggested for the natural experiment without premeasurement, as can be seen by glancing back at Table 6–2. Other designs which do use control groups, such as the natural experiment and the true experiment, might be preferred because they require less difficult assumptions. Unfortunately, these designs can be used only when the researcher has much more control over the subjects he is studying than most political scientists can achieve.

In order to use a natural experiment design, for instance, the researcher must be able to anticipate the occurrence of the test factor. He also must go to the expense in time and money of making two measurements of the subjects. Even then, he may have bad luck; for example, it may be that the test factor (especially if it is one which affects only a small part of the population) will have missed all but a few of the people he has included in his study. That is, he might be left with a control group but no test group.

Many important variables in the social sciences, therefore, are not at all susceptible to study by natural experiments. Some lie in the past—people's experiences during the Depression, the colonial histories of nations, the educational backgrounds and past professions of Congressmen, and so on. Others, such as assassinations, riots, and changes in the business cycle, are unpredictable. Such variables are very difficult to fit into a natural experiment design. On the other hand, some events are more easily anticipated— the introduction of a poverty program in a town, high school graduates' entrance into college, regularly scheduled political events such as elections, and so on. These lend themselves more readily to a natural experimental design.

A true experiment requires even greater control over the subjects of the study than does a natural experiment. The latter requires only that the investigator be able to anticipate events, but the true experiment requires that he be able to manipulate those events, for he must decide who is to fall into the control group and who is to fall into the experimental group. To do this in a field situation requires power over people in their normal lives, and it is no accident that the example of a true experiment which I used above, "Presidential lobbying," was carried out by the President. It is rare in real political situations that a researcher can have this kind of control over events.

It may be that in a small organization, such as a local political organization, or a portion of a campus, the investigator can carry out a true experimental design. For instance, students might conduct a political campaign among a randomly selected portion of the campus community, and compare that portion over time with a randomly selected control. The true experiment also has been attempted on a much larger scale, in at least one study.

Robert Agger and several East European colleagues have reported a bold attempt at a large political experiment, an attempt to measure the impact of adult educational and "politicizing" campaigns on various political and social attitudes.[9] In each of several countries, two similar towns were to be picked and the political attitudes of the citizens in each measured. Then a broad educational program was to be instituted in one of the two towns in each country. The citizens' attitudes would again be measured after the programs had been in operation for a period of time.

Other than rare examples such as this, true experimentation in political science is restricted to small-group studies dealing with artificial political situations. (For example, a group of subjects may be placed together and told to reach a decision on some question. The investigator then manipulates the way individuals in the group may communicate with each other, in order to see how this influences the result.) In such studies, of course, true experiments are the most appropriate design, inasmuch as the investigator generally can control all the relevant variables.

Because studies of this kind allow the investigator to use powerful experimental designs, they are potentially quite valuable. The main problem in working with them lies in applying the results from the contrived experimental situation to real politics. It is difficult to create an accurate approximation of real politics in an experiment, simply because the personal stakes in real politics are usually so high. It is one thing for a student playing "Nation A" to declare war on "Nation B" in an artificial experiment; it is quite another for the leader of one nation to declare war on another. It was once suggested, only half-seriously, that each of the subjects in such an experiment be given a pet dog which would be killed if he lost a war. This would presumably have raised the stakes in the experimental situation to approximate more closely those faced by the leaders of real nations.

Despite this problem, experimentation is potentially a very powerful tool for political research. It is probably most useful when the researcher is addressing basic decision-processes in a pure form (such as, "How do differences in power affect negotiating strategies?" "What effect does lack of information have on the level of tension in confrontations?" and so on). Here the problem of artificiality is greatly reduced, because it is not the researcher's intent to simulate directly any specific political situation.

THE USE OF VARIED DESIGNS AND MEASURES

I suppose the easiest conclusion to draw from the discussion above is that any kind of research in political science is difficult and that the results of political research are in the last analysis unreliable. But this would be far too sour a conclusion. I did not discuss these selected research designs in order

[9] Agger, Disman, Mlinar, and Sultanovic, 1970.

to convince you not to do political research, but to show you some of the problems you must deal with.

Even if you are forced to rely solely upon one of the weaker designs (operating without a control group, or using a control group with no pre-measurement), you are better off if you formally set out your design and measure those variables that can be measured, acknowledge alternative causal interpretations, and try to assess just how likely it is that each alternative is true. The choice is between doing this or giving up and relying on your intuition and impressions.

But there is a more hopeful side to this chapter. The very discussion of the weaknesses of various designs should suggest a solution: *wherever possible we should try to work simultaneously with a variety of designs, which can at least in part cancel out each other's weaknesses.* For example, in working solely with a contrived experiment, we may wonder whether the result we have obtained might be a result of something about the way the experiment was set up, rather than a "true" result. Working just with a natural experiment, we might wonder whether the result we have gotten could be a result of unusual people ending up in the test group, rather than a "true" result. But if we could use both of these designs, employing either the same or closely related measures, each result would bolster the other. We could be much more confident of the experimental result if we had gotten a similar result in a field situation. And we could be much more confident of the result of the natural experiment if we had gotten a similar result in an artificial true experiment.

If we can mix research strategies in this way, the end result is more than the sum of its parts. The strengths of the various designs complement each other. The likelihood that the alternative explanations associated with each design are true decreases because of the successful result from the other design. It seems less likely to us that the result of the natural experiment is due to unusual people entering the test group, for example, if similar results were obtained in a true experiment, in which entrance into the test group was controlled.

Note that the effect would not be the same if a single research design were repeated twice—if, say, a natural experiment were repeated in a different locality. To be sure, this should increase our confidence in the result somewhat, but not by as much as mixing designs did. Repeating the same design twice would increase our confidence only by showing us that the first result was not an accident or a result of the particular locality chosen. But the alternative causal interpretations which are associated with natural experimental design would in no way be weakened by the successful repetition. Consider the "Organizing the Poor" example once again. If the campaign in one city tended to reach mainly those who were already becoming more interested in politics, thus creating the illusion that the campaign had gotten them interested in politics, there is no reason to think that a similar campaign would not do the same thing in a second city. Getting the same result in two different cities would not make it any less likely that the alternative causal interpretation was true.

AN EXAMPLE OF VARIED DESIGNS AND MEASURES

Robert E. Lane, in "The Politics of Consensus in an Age of Affluence," uses the varied-design strategy rather well.[10] His study is worth going into at some length as an extended example. Lane wanted to test the general hypothesis that with the greater prosperity of a modern economy, tensions and conflicts between groups would decrease and politics would be based increasingly on trust and mutual interests. The paper was written sometime before 1965, and although its conclusion has since proved false in at least the short run, Lane produced strong evidence at that time that the hypothesis was true.

His problem in the paper was much like that in my earlier example, "Spock Revolution." He wanted to show that the increasing *prosperity* of the United States and the increasing *economic security* for individuals resulting from the dampening of the business cycle had caused an increase in trust between groups and a relaxation of political tensions. He first had to show that there had in fact been a trend over the previous couple of decades toward greater trust and more relaxed politics. Because these are difficult concepts to measure, and the validity of single indicators of either one would be suspect, he used a surprising number of indicators. To name just a few, he included answers to such questions as: "Would you vote for a Jew for President?" "How happy are you?" "Does it make much difference to you which party wins the election?" and "Do you consider the amount of tax you pay too high?" Twenty-two such questions were used in all, and a good deal of ingenuity went into connecting some of them to the things they were to measure. In almost all of them Lane was able to show similar trends toward greater trust and relaxation. The total effect of this battery of indicators is rather convincing.

Now he was faced with the same problem as in "Spock Revolution." The two trends had indeed coincided, but how could he show that the trend in the economy, and not something else, had caused the trend in trust and conflict? There was no control group readily available; the entire country was involved in the economic trend.

He handled the problem in part simply by arguing that the trend in the economy was the most reasonable thing to have caused the trend in trust. This is a key part of interpretation—simply justifying, on logical or other grounds, the reasonableness of the particular causal interpretation you

[10] Lane, 1965.

choose. (Remember, there is always an element of subjectivity in causal interpretations.)

Beyond this, however, Lane was able to add a similar analysis, using a control group with no premeasurement design. He compared answers from several countries to a question on how important people found the differences between political parties. He found that the richer the country, the more its citizens tended to minimize the differences between political parties. This added strength to his conviction that it was not "something else" which had happened to the United States over the previous two decades that had led to the trend in trust and conflict there.

It is possible that Lane could have varied his research designs even more than he did. For one thing, internal comparisons of people in different economic situations in the United States might have provided him with some additional control group with no premeasurement analyses. He could have compared people with different incomes and also people whose occupations insured varying degrees of stability in incomes. In addition to adding further evidence that it was not "something else" that caused the trend in trust and conflict, this strategy would have allowed him to sort out the effects of "prosperity" and "economic security," which are hopelessly intertwined in looking at gross national figures. Lane cannot really tell from his study whether the trend he sees is more a result of prosperity or of security, although he argues in the abstract that it is likely to be a result of both. During the postwar period, both the level of income and the security of that income rose in the United States, so their effects cannot be separated. The same is probably true of the five nations he compared. The richer nations probably are also the ones in which there is greater economic security. But in comparing people with different occupations within the United States, Lane could have gotten all sorts of combinations of security and level of income. Some jobs, such as bank teller, are secure but low-paid; others, such as acting, large-scale truck farming, or stock speculation, may be very well-paid but are insecure; and of course, many jobs are low-paid and insecure or well-paid and secure.

Lane might have found that how trusting a person was and what his attitude toward conflict was did not vary much from one occupation to another. This would have suggested that it might indeed have been "something else" that caused the trends he observed in the country as whole, inasmuch as an analysis with a control group produced a different result. He might have found that these attitudes varied with the income of the occupation but not the security, which would have suggested that his trend was due to the growth in income, not to the growth in security. He might have found that they varied with the security of the occupation but not the income, which would have suggested that his trend was due to the growth in security alone. Or, of course, he might have found that they varied with both income and security independently, which would have confirmed his general assumptions, as well as strengthening his design.[11]

Lane also might have devised a natural experiment to complement his other research designs. It sometimes happens that survey research is carried on with a "panel," a group of people who are interviewed once and then interviewed again at a later time to see how they have changed. Had Lane obtained the results of research in which such a panel answered questions relevant to his study, he might have treated the first questioning period as the premeasurement, the respondents' economic experiences between questioning periods as the test factor, and the second questioning period as the postmeasurement.

If he had gotten the same result in all of these varied tests, each with its own weaknesses partially canceled out by the other results, Lane would have had a more convincing study. As it is, his varied set of research designs, and especially of measures, makes a rather convincing case.

CONCLUSION

To pick up once again the refrain of this book, creativity and originality lie at the heart of elegant research. Anybody—or almost anybody—can take a research problem, carry out a fairly obvious test on it, using one or two obvious measures, and either ignore or assume away the ever-present alternative causal interpretations. A creative researcher will not be satisfied with this, but will try very hard to account for all the alternative interpretations of his findings. He will muster logical arguments; he will cite evidence from related studies; he may vary the designs and measures in his own study. All of these techniques will help him to limit the number of plausible alternative interpretations of his findings.

The suggestion I made above—to vary measures and designs—is, I think, a useful one, but it should not be thought of as the one answer. It is generally useful, if possible, to vary designs, but there are other ways to eliminate alternative interpretations—such as by logical argument or by indirect evidence of various sorts. No interpretation of a research result is cut-and-dried; interpreting a result and handling alternative interpretations of the result are a difficult and challenging part of research.

HOLDING A VARIABLE CONSTANT

I have talked about "holding a variable constant" more than once in this chapter. If we want to know whether a relationship between two variables can be accounted for by a third variable which is related

---

[11] Note that the treatment of occupations which I suggest here is an example of the "enriched measurement" which I urged in Chapter 5. A set of nominal categories, "occupation," is used simultaneously as indicators for two ordinal scales, "level of income" and "security of income."

Table 6-3

	Urban	Rural	Total
Support	75	48	123
Do Not Support	45	82	127
Total	120	130	250

to both of them, we can "hold constant" the third variable to see whether the relationship between the first two continues to exist when the third variable is not free to vary. "Holding a variable constant" is often also called "controlling for the variable."

The simplest way to do this is to divide the subjects into separate groups, each having a distinct value on the variable to be held constant, and then observe whether in each of these groups there is a relationship between the first two variables. If there is, it cannot be due to variation in the third variable, for within each of these groups the third variable literally is constant.

Consider the hypothetical figures in Table 6–3, relating legislators' constituencies in a certain state (urban or rural) to the legislators' support for the governor's poverty bill.

Table 6–3 shows a relationship between the two variables; 62.5 percent of the urban legislators (75/120) support the governor's bill compared with 36.9 percent of the rural legislators (48/130). However, a skeptic might point out that it is because the governor is a Democrat and the urban representatives tend to be Democratic that this relationship appears. In other words, there might be nothing *per se* about an urban representative that makes him vote for the poverty bill. Democrats might tend to be urban and also tend to support the governor, thus making it appear that urban representatives favor the bill more than rural representatives.

To test this alternative explanation of the relationship, we can separate the representatives into Democrats and Republicans, as in Tables 6–4A and 6–4B, and look at each of these groups separately.

From these tables, we can see that the alternative explanation is correct. If party does not vary (and we have made certain that it does not vary within each of these groups), there is no relationship between the variables. Among the Democrats, 80 percent of the urban representatives support the bill; so do 80 percent of the rural representatives. Among Republicans, 10 percent of the urban representatives favor the bill, as do 10 percent of the rural representatives.

Table 6–4A   Democrats

	Urban	Rural	Total
Support	72	40	112
Do Not Support	18	10	28
Total	90	50	140

Table 6–4B   Republicans

	Urban	Rural	Total
Support	3	8	11
Do Not Support	27	72	99
Total	30	80	110

The result could have turned out differently, as in Tables 6–5A and 6–5B. In Tables 6–5A and 6–5B, even though party is a constant within each table, the relationship persists. Among the Democrats, 66.7 percent of the urban representatives support the bill, compared with 33.3 percent of the rural representatives. Among Republicans, 58.3 percent of the urban representatives support the bill, compared with 38.0 percent of the rural representatives. In this case, there *is* something about the urban and rural representatives, other than their party, that causes them to vote differently on the poverty bill.

Table 6–5A   Democrats

	Urban	Rural	Total
Support	40	10	50
Do Not Suuport	20	20	40
Total	60	30	90

Table 6–5B   Republicans

	Urban	Rural	Total
Support	35	38	73
Do Not Support	25	62	87
Total	60	100	160

The technique which I have used here to hold a variable constant—literally separating the subjects into new little groups and doing the same analysis within each of these groups—is the simplest technique which can be used. There are also statistical techniques such as multiple regression which *artificially* hold variables constant, and the effect of these techniques is approximately the same as the direct technique I used here.[12] The advantage of such statistical techniques is that they can conveniently hold several variables constant simultaneously. Doing this with the direct technique would not be easy. First of all, it would result in a horrendous number of tiny tables. More seriously, many of these would be based on a quite small number of cases, and their meaning would thus be uncertain.

FURTHER DISCUSSION

I have presented here only a few examples of the more commonly used research designs. I also have dealt with only a sample of the possible alternative explanations which may apply to different designs. A more complete treatment of research design, excellent and readable, is provided in Campbell and Stanley, *Experimental and Quasi-Experimental Designs for Research* (Rand McNally & Co., 1963). I have relied heavily on their approach in this chapter. A good treatment of the concept of "cause" in relation to research design is found in Blalock, 1964, Chaps. 1 and 2. An example of unusually careful and creative interpretations, operating under circumstances in which research designs were quite limited, is Tingsten, 1937. Several interesting examples of improvised research designs in field research on animal behavior can be found in Tinbergen, 1968.

One question you might consider in connection with this chapter is: Why should theory-oriented, empirical political research be based almost exclusively on causal relationships, rather than on relationships in general?

---

[12] See Chapter 7 for an elementary discussion of multiple regression.

INTRODUCTION TO STATISTICS

MEASURING RELATIONSHIPS FOR INTERVAL DATA

7

In Chapter 6 we were concerned generally with "relationships" between independent and dependent variables. That is, we wanted to see whether the presence or absence of a test factor affected the value of the dependent variable.

This was too simple, for two reasons. First of all, as noted in footnote 8 in that chapter, the test factor in field research is frequently not something which is simply present or absent; rather, it takes on a variety of values. Our task then is not just to see whether the *presence or absence* of a test factor affects the value of the dependent variable, but instead to see whether the *value* of the independent variable affects the value of the dependent variable. For example, in relating education to income, we do not treat people simply as "educated" or "not educated." They have varying amounts of education, and our task is to see whether the amount of education each individual has affects his income.

Secondly, "relationship" cannot be dichotomized, although I treated it as a dichotomy in Chapter 6, in order to ease the presentation there. Two variables are not simply "related" or "not related." Relationships vary in two ways. (1) They vary in how *strongly* the independent variable affects the dependent variable. For instance, education might have only a minor effect on income. The average income of college graduates might be $11,000 and the average income of high school dropouts might be $10,000. Or, it might have a major effect. College graduates might average $20,000 while high school dropouts average $6,000.

(2) Relationships also vary in how *completely* the independent variable determines scores on the dependent variable. College graduates might average $20,000 income and high school dropouts $6,000, for instance, and yet there still be much variation in incomes which could not be attributed to variation in people's education. Some college graduates might make only

$5,000 a year and some high school dropouts might make $40,000 or $50,000 a year, even though the *average* income of the college graduates was higher than the *average* income of the dropouts. This would indicate that although education affected incomes sharply, it was relatively incomplete as an explanation of people's incomes. Because income still varied a good deal within each level of the independent variable, there must be other things affecting income in important ways, and we often would guess incorrectly if we tried to predict an individual's income solely from his education. This is what it means to say that education is not a very "complete" explanation of income.

Thus, variables are not simply "related" or "not related." Their relationship may be such that the independent variable has a *greater or lesser effect* on the dependent variable; and it may be such that the independent variable determines the dependent variable *more or less completely*. In general in political research, we are not concerned simply with whether or not two variables are related, but with whether or not they have a "strong" relationship (in one or both of the senses used above). This can be seen by looking back at the examples of research design in the preceding chapter. Although for the sake of simplicity these were presented as if we wanted to test whether or not a relationship existed, it is clear that what was of interest to the investigators in each case was finding out how *strong* a relationship existed. In "Presidential lobbying," for instance, the President was not simply concerned with whether or not he was able to affect votes on the bill, but with *how many* votes he could swing.

Our task in evaluating the results of research, then, is to measure how strong a relationship exists between the independent variable(s) and the dependent variable. The tools we need in order to do this are found in the field of statistics.

STATISTICS Although modern political scientists have only recently begun to use statistics extensively, it was actually political scientists of a sort who first developed the field, for statistics originally grew out of the need to keep records for the state. The name "statistics," in fact, derives from the Latin *statisticus*, "of state affairs."

Statistics includes two main activities: statistical inference and statistical measurement (including the measurement of relationships, with which we shall be concerned in this chapter). Statistical inference consists of estimating how likely it is that we could have gotten a particular result by chance; in a sense it tells us how reliable the results of our research are. I shall discuss inference in Chapter 9. In this chapter, and in Chapter 8, I shall introduce some statistical techniques for measuring the strength of relationships.

THE IMPORTANCE OF LEVELS OF MEASUREMENT

We saw in Chapter 5 that we have more information about a relationship between variables if we work at a higher level of measurement than we do if we work at a lower level of measurement. It should not be too surprising that methods of measuring relationships between variables are different depending on the level at which the variables were measured. If we know more about a relationship, we should be able to measure a greater variety of things about it. Just as higher levels of measurement give relatively richer information about a variable, techniques for measuring relationships that are appropriate for a high level of measurement give relatively richer information about a relationship.

The most important difference of this sort separates those techniques that are appropriate for data measured at the interval from those that are appropriate for data measured at a lower level. I suggested above that there are two ways in which we can measure the "strength" of a relationship between two variables. (1) We can measure how great a difference the independent variable makes in the dependent variable; that is, we can see how greatly values of the dependent variable differ, given varying scores on the independent variable. Or, (2) we can measure how completely the dependent variable is determined by the independent variable; that is, we can measure the degree of accuracy with which scores on the dependent variable may be predicted from scores on the independent variable (how complete an explanation of the dependent variable is provided by the independent variable). I shall call the first way of measuring a relationship "*effect-descriptive*," and the second "*correlational*." The critical difference between working with interval-measured data and working with data measured at a lower level is that "effect-descriptive" measurement can apply only to interval-scale data. "Correlational" measurement of one sort or another can apply to data measured at any level.

Thinking back to the nature of ordinal and nominal measurement, it should be clear that for these levels of measurement we cannot tell how great a difference in the dependent variable is produced by a given difference in values of the independent variable, although this is what we must do to measure the relationship in an "effect-descriptive" way. The whole point of nominal and ordinal measurement is that in neither do we know the actual values of the variable; therefore, we cannot measure a *difference* in the values. If we are using an ordinal-scale variable we know whether one value is higher than another, but we do not know how much higher it is. If we are using a nominal-scale variable, of course, all we know is whether the two values are distinct.

This becomes a particularly important distinction in political research, because under most circumstances, "effect-descriptive" ways of measuring the strength of a relationship are more useful than "correlational" ways. I shall try to demonstrate this in the next few sections.

WORKING WITH
INTERVAL DATA

REGRESSION ANALYSIS

A convenient way to summarize data on two interval-scale variables, so that we can easily see what is going on in the relationship between them, is by plotting all of the observations on a "scattergram," as in Figure 7–1. Each dot in the scattergram represents one observation (a person, state, country, or what have you), placed in the graph according to its scores on the two variables. For instance, dot A represents an observation which combines scores of 2 on the independent variable and 3 on the dependent variable. Dot B represents an observation with scores of 8 on the independent variable and 12 on the dependent variable.

By looking at the pattern in the dots, we can tell a good deal about the relationship between the two variables. For instance, in Figure 7–1, we note that there are few dots in the lower-right and upper-left corners of the graph. This means that high scores on the dependent variable tend to coincide with high scores on the independent variable, and low scores on the dependent

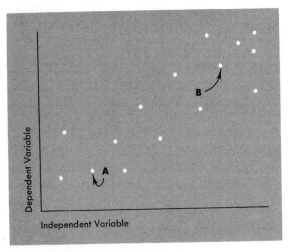

Figure 7–1 A Scattergram

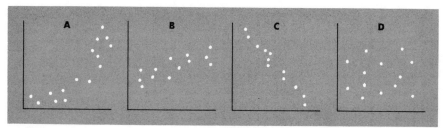

Figure 7–2   Assorted Scattergrams

variable tend to coincide with low scores on the independent variable. Thus, we know that the two variables are positively related. Furthermore, this relationship appears to be approximately linear. (See the discussion of "linear relationships" in the box on page 74.)

We have done two things so far. We have observed which way the dependent variable moves with changes in the independent variable, and we have observed that it moves at a steady rate at all values of the independent variable (a linear relationship), rather than at changing rates (a nonlinear relationship). These are both part of an "effect-descriptive" measurement of the relationship.

The scattergrams in Figure 7–2 illustrate various other patterns which we might have observed. Graph A shows a nonlinear relationship (the dependent variable increases faster with increases in the independent variable if the independent variable has a high value). Graph B shows a linear relationship in which the dependent variable increases more gradually than in the graph in Figure 7–1. Graph C shows a negative linear relationship in which the dependent variable decreases as the independent variable increases. And graph D shows a pattern in which there is no relationship.

Although the scattergram tells us a good deal about the relationship, it can be unwieldy to work with. It is not uncommon in a research report to discuss thirty or forty separate relationships. It would be painful to read such a paper if each relationship were presented in the form of a scattergram. What is more, comparing two scattergrams gives us only an approximate idea of the differences between two relationships. Comparing the graphs in Figures 7–1 and 7–2 (B), we can say that in the first graph the independent variable causes greater shifts in the dependent variable than in the second, but we cannot say precisely how much greater the shifts are. And if the differences were more subtle, or if we were comparing several relationships, the job would be more difficult still.

Finally and most importantly, we often measure the strength of a relationship between two variables, holding a third variable constant. (See

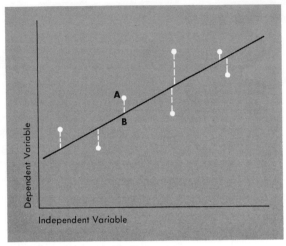

Figure 7–3   The Regression Line

the discussion of "holding a variable constant," pages 98–102. This may be impossible to do using scattergrams.

For all of these reasons, it is useful to devise a precise numerical measure which will summarize the relevant characteristics of the relationship shown in a scattergram. The measure commonly used to summarize the "effect-descriptive" characteristics of a scattergram is the "regression coefficient."

The linear regression coefficient is derived in the following way. First, the pattern in the dots of the scattergram is summed up by a single line which best traces the pattern. If the relationship is linear, this can be a straight line, which simplifies the analysis considerably. It has been found that the mathematically best procedure is to choose the line which minimizes the squared differences between observed values of the dependent variable and the idealized values of the dependent variable on the simplifying line. This is illustrated in Figure 7–3.

In Figure 7–3 a simplifying line has been drawn through a scattergram with seven observations to summarize the pattern in the dots. It has been drawn such that it minimizes the squared differences between each of the observed points, such as A, and the point B at which an observation having A's score on the independent variable would be expected to fall on the idealized simplifying line.

The simplifying line may be thought of as a rule for predicting scores on the dependent variable from scores on the independent variable. In this sense, it is set up in such a way that the average squared value of the "mistake" one would make in predicting scores on the dependent variable is kept as low as possible.

A single summarizing line can be described more easily than a pattern of dots. In particular, being in this case a straight line, it can be fully described by the equation:

$$y = a + bx,$$

where y is the predicted value of the dependent variable, x is the value of the independent variable, and "a" and "b" are numbers relating y to x. The number "a" is the expected value of y when x equals zero, and is called the *intercept* of the regression equation; it is the value of y where the regression line crosses the y axis, where x equals zero. (See Figure 7–4.) The number "b," or the *slope* of the regression equation, shows by how many units y increases as x increases one unit. (If b is negative, then y decreases as x increases; there is a negative relationship between the variables.) In other words, to find the predicted value of the dependent variable for any specified value of the independent variable, you must add "a" (the predicted value of y when x equals zero) to "b" times the number of units by which x exceeds zero.

The slope, often simply called the *regression coefficient*, is the most valuable part of this equation for most purposes in the social sciences. By telling how great a shift we can expect in the dependent variable if the independent variable shifts by one unit, it provides a single, precise sum-

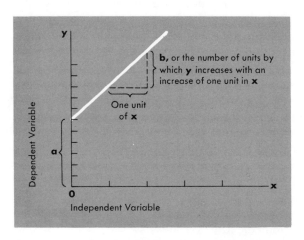

Figure 7–4 The Regression Equation. The equation of this line is
y = 6 + 3x. The predicted value of y when x is four,
for instance, is 6 + (4 × 3), or 18.

mary measure of how great an impact the independent variable has on the dependent variable. For instance, if the relationship between income and electoral participation is linear and can be summarized by the regression equation:

percent voting $= 50.5 + 3$ (income in thousands of dollars),

this means that with every additional thousand dollars of income, three percent more potential voters vote.

Remember, however, that even though we work with neat, impersonal numbers, we do not escape the scholar's obligation to think. If we have guessed the direction of causation between x and y incorrectly, plugging in our data and getting numbers out will not make our results valid. If y causes x, rather than vice versa, the formulas will still give us an "a" and a "b," but the shift of one unit in x in the real world will *not* be followed by a shift of b units in y. Thus, the arguments made in Chapter 6 apply just the same, even when we work with these simple numbers. One danger of working with such summary numbers is that it is so easy to plug the numbers in and forget to think.

The Problem of Comparing Units   It may be seen from this geometric interpretation of the slope (the number of units by which y changes with a change of one unit in x), that the slope has meaning only with regard to the units in which x and y are measured. For example, if there is a regression coefficient of -10.5 for nations' diplomatic involvement with the United States (measured by the number or magnitude of exchanges per year) predicted from their distance from the United States measured in thousands of miles, there would be a regression coefficient of -0.0105 for the same dependent variable predicted from distance measured in miles. That is, if diplomatic involvement could be expected to decrease by 10.5 with every thousand miles of distance from the United States, it would be expected to decrease by 0.0105 with every mile of distance.

If we are working with just two variables, this poses no real difficulty. But often we may be interested in comparing the effects of two or more independent variables on a particular dependent variable. If the two independent variables are measured in different sorts of units, this can be difficult. Continuing with the example above, we might want to know which variable—nations' distance from the United States, or the volume of their trade with the United States—has a greater impact on their diplomatic interaction with the United States. If the regression coefficient for volume of trade, measured in millions of dollars, is $+0.024$, how can we tell whether it has a greater impact on diplomatic interaction than does geographic distance, with its slope of -10.5? The units—thousands of miles and millions of dollars—are not comparable; therefore the coefficients based on those units are not comparable either.

Checking for Linearity   We must be careful to make certain in using linear regression analysis that the data do fit a more or less linear pattern. Otherwise, the regression equation will not summarize the pattern in the data, but will distort it. Figure 7–5 shows a linear regression equation passed through the scattergram of a nonlinear relationship. This regression line fits the data very badly and is not a useful summary of what is going on in them. You should always check your data before using linear regression analysis. The best way to do this is simply to draw a scattergram (or better yet, let the computer do it for you), and see whether it looks linear.

Many relationships in political science do turn out to be linear. But if the relationship you are interested turns out to be nonlinear, that is no reason to give up analyzing it. It merely means that the relationship is more complicated—and probably more interesting. A nonlinear regression equation may be found which fits the pattern in the data fairly well.

In Figure 7–6, a nonlinear regression equation $a + b_1x - b_2x^2$ has been passed through the scattergram from Figure 7–5. It summarizes the pattern in the data accurately. In this case, two coefficients, b_1 and b_2, are required to express the impact that a change in x will have on y, inasmuch as that change is not the same at all values of x. We can see that y increases with x,

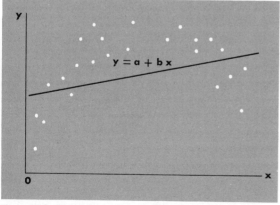

Figure 7–5   Linear Regression on a Nonlinear Relationship

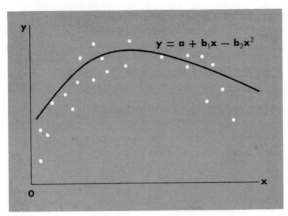

Figure 7–6   A Nonlinear Regression Equation

but decreases with the square of x. The regression equation provides a handy summary description of the effect, now a bit more complicated, that x has on y.

Formulas are available to calculate equations for regression lines satisfying the least squares criteria. This is particularly true for linear regression; the formulas for a and b are found in every standard statistics text, including the ones cited at the end of this chapter. But there are no set "formulas" for nonlinear regression equations, for there is an infinite variety of nonlinear equations which you might fit to any set of data. It usually is necessary to play around with alternative nonlinear equations for a while. But these, too, can be worked out readily enough. One important warning: Remember that the presentation that I have made here is only a broad, introductory overview. Competence in using measures like those presented here requires more thorough training than is within the scope of this book.

Examining the Residuals   Any regression line is calculated as a result of whatever state we are presently at in developing a theory. Because our theory anticipates a relationship between two variables, we measure the relationship between them by calculating the regression equation for the line which best summarizes the pattern of the relationship. In this sense, regression analysis is an expression of what we already think about the subject. It may surprise us; where we expected a relationship there may be none, or it may be nonlinear, and so on. But it is an expression of what we already have been thinking about the subject.

However, the regression line can serve an equally important function in helping us develop our theory further, by pointing out important inde-

pendent variables which had not occurred to us. Looking back at Figure 7–3, note that the regression line does not provide perfect prediction of the values on the dependent variable for the cases in the scattergram. This means there is still variation in the dependent variable which is unexplained, even when we take the independent variable into account. Some of the observations are higher on the dependent variable than we would expect from their value on the independent variable, and some are lower. *Something else, beyond the independent variable, is affecting the dependent variable.*

The difference between the observed value and the predicted value is called the *residual.* Examining these residuals points out to us those cases in which the "something else" has the effect of raising the dependent variable, and those in which it has the effect of lowering the dependent variable. In Figure 7–3, for instance, a case such as A is one in which the effect of the "something else" is to raise the value of the dependent variable; the actual value for case A is higher than the value B which would have been predicted from the regression line for a case with A's value on the independent variable.

Now, once the cases have been sorted out in this way, we may notice that cases with similar residuals have some additional characteristic in common. This can then point up an additional variable which may be brought into our theory. Suppose, for instance, that in Figure 7–3 the independent variable were countries' gross national products and the dependent variable were the percentages of their budgets spent on education. On examining the residuals, you might notice that all of the countries for which educational spending was higher than predicted were democracies, and all of the countries for which it was unexpectedly low were not democracies. In this way you might discover the identity of the "something else," beyond GNP, which was needed for your theory. Notice that it would have been difficult to see this, if you had not first regressed educational spending on GNP and then looked at the residuals. The richest nondemocracies of Figure 7–3 show a higher rate of educational spending than do the poorest democracies. It might not have been at all obvious that "democracy" was a variable you should use to explain levels of educational spending.

The technique of examining residuals is illustrated in Figure 7–7, adapted from V. O. Key, Jr.'s *Southern Politics.*[1] Key wanted to measure the impact of factions in Alabama primaries. He related counties' votes for Folsom, a progressive candidate in the 1946 gubernatorial primary, to their votes for Sparkman, a progressive candidate in the 1946 senatorial primary. He found a moderately strong relationship between the two.

Because this meant that counties tended to lean the same way in both

[1] Key, 1950, p. 48.

elections, it indicated the presence of conservative and progressive factions structuring the vote, as Key had expected. Had such factions not existed, there would have been no particular reason to expect a county to vote in much the same way in the two primaries. But the relationship was not very tight. Many counties, such as the one which gave 90 percent of its vote to Folsom and 45 percent to Sparkman, voted far differently than one would have expected simply on the basis of conservative and progressive factions. This indicated the presence of other variables, which were causing additional variations in the vote.

By examining the residuals around the regression line, Key got some

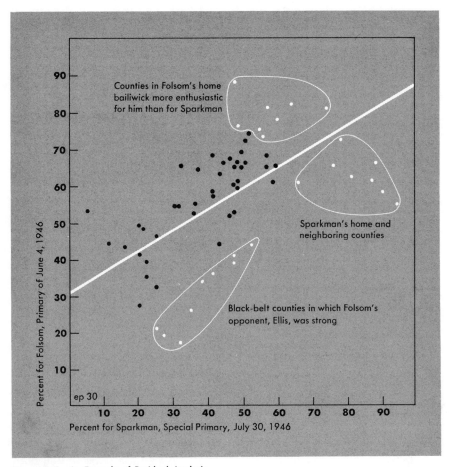

Figure 7–7   An Example of Residual Analysis

Source: V. O. Key, Jr., Southern Politics (New York: Alfred A. Knopf, Inc., 1950), p. 48.

idea of what these variables might be. In this case, it turned out that the residuals could be explained in part by the effect of "friends and neighbors." Counties in Folsom's home part of the state voted for him more enthusiastically than would have been expected on the basis of their vote for Sparkman. Counties in Sparkman's home part of the state voted less enthusiastically for Folsom than would have been expected from their vote for Sparkman (which presumably was high because he was a local boy). Similarly, the "home" counties of Folsom's opponent went less heavily for Folsom than would have been expected on the basis of their vote for Sparkman. This pointed out to Key the importance of local solidarity, one of the major forces retarding the development of stable statewide factions in Alabama politics at that time. Much of the looseness in the relationship between the votes for two candidates of the same faction was shown to be a result of people's tendency to vote for a candidate on the basis of where he came from in the state, rather than the faction with which he was identified.

Users of regression analysis in political science far too rarely go on to the creative and exploratory labor of examining the residuals to see what additional variables affect the dependent variable. Usually the spread of dots around the regression line is treated as an act of God, or as a measure of the basic uncertainty of human affairs. In fact, it is a trove in which new variables lie waiting to be discovered. I suspect the reason most of us do not go on to examine this trove is that we have developed a proprietorial sense toward our theories before we ever get to the point of testing them. There is a certain completeness about one's own theory, and it does not occur to us to use our theory as a "mere" starting point in the search for explanations.

CORRELATION ANALYSIS

At the beginning of this chapter, I pointed out that there are two ways in which we can measure the strength of a relationship—by measuring how much difference the independent variable makes in the dependent variable, and by measuring how completely the independent variable determines the dependent variable. For interval scale data, the regression coefficient accomplishes the first of these; the correlation coefficient accomplishes the second.

Consider the graphs in Figure 7–8. Both relationships can be summarized by the same regression line, but the value of the dependent variable in graph B is less closely determined by the independent variable than in graph A. A change in the independent variable tends to produce the same change in the dependent variable, on the average, in both graphs. But this tendency is weaker, and more likely to be disturbed by "other factors" in graph B; the residuals tend to be larger in graph B than in graph A. In

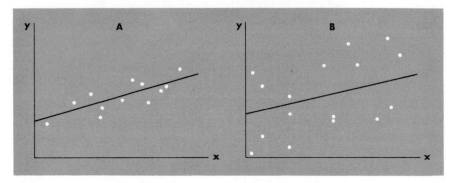

Figure 7–8   Two Correlations

one sense, then, the relationship in graph B is weaker than the relationship in graph A, because the dependent variable is less a result of the independent variable, compared to "other factors" (the unknown things that cause the residuals to exist), in B than in A.

The *product-moment correlation coefficient,* r, measures how widely such a body of data spreads around a regression line. This coefficient compares a set of data with ideal models of a perfect relationship and a perfect lack of relationship, and assigns to the relationship a score ranging in absolute value from zero to one, depending on how closely the data approximate a perfect relationship. The two extreme models are illustrated in Figure 7–9.

In graph A of Figure 7–9, the data all fall on a straight line through the scattergram. A regression line passed through them would leave no residual variation at all in the dependent variable: Thus, the independent

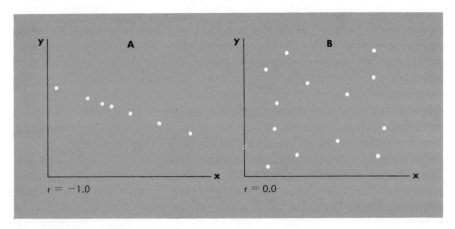

Figure 7–9   Extreme Models of Correlation

variable determines the dependent variable completely. The correlation co-efficient for this type has an absolute value of one.

In graph B, values of the dependent variable are combined randomly with values of the independent variable, so that any given value of the dependent variable is as likely to coincide with a low value on the inde-pendent variable as with a high one. Thus, there is no pattern to the relation-ship. This indicates that the independent variable has no effect on the dependent variable. The correlation coefficient for this type has absolute value zero.

Most relationships, of course, fall somewhere between these two ex-tremes; the closer a relationship approaches the situation in graph A, the higher its correlation coefficient will be in absolute value. Thus, the correla-tion coefficient provides a measure by which the strengths of various rela-tionships can be compared, in the *correlational* sense of "strength of relationship."

I have referred here only to the absolute value of the correlation co-efficient. In addition to showing how closely a relationship approaches the situation in graph A, the correlation coefficient indicates by its sign whether the relationship is positive or negative. The coefficient ranges from −1.0 (a perfect negative relationship, such as the one in graph A) through 0.0 to +1.0 (a perfect positive relationship, similar to the one in graph A but tilted up). In a positive relationship, increases in the independent variable produce increases in the dependent variable; in a negative relationship, in-creases in the independent variable produce decreases in the dependent variable.

Interpreting the Correlation Coefficient   Although it is clear enough what correlation coefficients of −1, 0, or +1 mean, there is no easy way of interpreting what coefficients between these values mean. It is true that the higher the absolute value of the coefficient, the closer it approaches the model in graph A, so that if we wish to compare two dif-ferent relationships, we can say which is stronger. But it is not easy to see what the difference between them means. It is *not* true, for instance, that the difference between r = .8 and r = .6 is the same as the difference be-tween r = .4 and r = .2. And it is also not true that r = −.6 is twice as strong as r = −.3. This is reminiscent of the difference between ordinal and inter-val measurement: we know that the higher the absolute value of r, the stronger the relationship; but we do not know *how much* stronger one rela-tionship is than another.

Fortunately, the *square* of the correlation coefficient (sometimes called the "coefficient of determination," but more often just r^2) does have a usable interpretation at all values of r. Before we can consider this, I must first introduce the concept of "variance."

Variance   The variance of a variable is the average squared deviation of values of that variable from their own mean.[2] For instance, if there are just three cases, with scores of -1, 4, and 5 for a variable, their mean is $(-1 + 4 + 5)/3 = 8/3$, and their variance is

$$\frac{(-1 - 8/3)^2 + (4 - 8/3)^2 + (5 - 8/3)^2}{3} =$$

$$\frac{(-11/3)^2 + (4/3)^2 + (7/3)^2}{3} =$$

$$\frac{121/9 + 16/9 + 49/9}{3} = 6.89$$

The formula for the variance of any variable x is:

$$\text{Variance}_x = \frac{\Sigma(x - \bar{x})^2}{N},$$

where $\bar{x}$ is the mean of x, and N is the number of observations we wish to average. The Σ sign simply means that for all the observations, we are to calculate $(x - \bar{x})^2$, and then add these results together. The expression $\Sigma (x - \bar{x})^2$ is equivalent to writing $(x_1 - \bar{x})^2 + (x_2 - \bar{x})^2 + \ldots + (x_N - \bar{x})^2$.

The variance is a measure of how widely the observed values of a variable vary among themselves. If they do not vary at all, but each has the same value, then the variance will be zero. This is true because each value will equal the mean, and thus the sum of the squared deviations from the mean will equal zero. The more the values vary among themselves, the further each will be from the mean of them all, and the greater the sum of squared deviations from the mean will be. Thus, the more they vary among themselves, the higher their variance will be.

The variance of the dependent variable, y, can be depicted in a scattergram by drawing a horizontal line at $y = \bar{y}$, and drawing in the residuals around this line, as in Figure 7–10. The average squared value of the residuals, because it is the average squared deviation of the values of y from their own mean, is the variance of y.

One useful way to look at our goal in theoretical social science research is to note that our task is to account for the variance in a dependent variable. It is the variance in something that puzzles us and challenges us to produce an explanation. Why is it that some people make more money than other people? That some nations are frequently involved in wars and others

---

[2] The "mean" of the variable is its arithmetic mean, or average—the sum of all the values, divided by the number of cases.

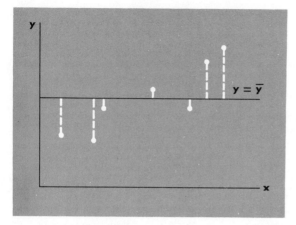

Figure 7–10   The Variance of y

are not? That some congressmen vote for a bill and others oppose it? That some people are more politically alienated than others? All of these questions simply ask: to what can the variance in this variable be attributed; *why does this variable vary?*

Comparing Figures 7–3 and 7–10, it should appear that there is at least a superficial similarity between the residuals around the least-squares line and the variance of the dependent variable. The least-squares line is a line passed through the scattergram in any direction such that the squared deviations of values of the dependent variable from that line are minimized. The line $y = \bar{y}$ is a *horizontal* line passed through the data in the scattergram, and inspection will suggest what is, in fact, mathematically true: this line is the one *horizontal* line which minimizes the squared deviations of values of the dependent variable from itself.[3] That is, any other horizontal line passed through the data would yield a greater sum of squared deviations in the dependent variable.

This similarity suggests that the squared deviations around the regression line may be treated as the variance of the dependent variable around the values predicted for the dependent variable by the regression equation. In the sense that I used it above, this is the variance in the dependent variable which is still left to be accounted for after we have taken into account the effect of the independent variable.

Thus, we have two variances for the dependent variable—its variance around its mean (the "total variance") and its variance around the regression line ("variance left unexplained by the independent variable"). To the

[3] See Blalock, 1960, p. 48.

extent that the dependent variable is determined by the independent variable, this unexplained variance will be small compared to the total variance. If the dependent variable can be predicted perfectly from the independent variable, as in Figure 7–9(A), then the unexplained variance will be zero. If the dependent variable is unrelated to the independent variable, as in Figure 7–9(B), then the regression line will be horizontal, indicating that the same value of the dependent variable is predicted at all values of the independent variable; in fact, inasmuch as the line $y = \bar{y}$ is the horizontal line which minimizes squared deviations around itself, the regression line will equal the line $y = \bar{y}$ in this case. Thus, the unexplained variance will equal the total variance.

Dividing the unexplained variance by the total variance tells us what proportion of the total variance is left, after we have allowed the independent variable to explain as much as it can explain. As it happens, r^2 equals one minus this proportion, or

$$1 - \frac{\text{unexplained variance}}{\text{total variance}},$$

that is, the proportion of the total variance in the dependent variable which is due to the independent variable.[4] This gives us a useful interpretation of r at all values. If you read that an author has found a correlation of $-.30$ between two variables, you should mentally square the correlation and interpret that statement: "the two variables are negatively related, and 9 percent of the variance in one is due to the other."

Another helpful way to look at this interpretation is to think in terms of prediction. Operating without any knowledge of the independent variable, our best strategy in trying to predict values of the dependent variable for particular cases would be to guess that the value in any given case is the mean. We would be less wrong more of the time than with any other guess we could make.[5] If we now add knowledge of the independent variable, our best guess becomes the value predicted from the regression equation. The magnitude of the mistakes in each case is now represented by squared deviations around the predictions. The value r^2 measures the proportion by which we have reduced our mistakes in predicting the dependent variable by introducing knowledge of the independent variable.

[4] For a good presentation of this interpretation, including the proof that

$$r^2 = 1 - \frac{\text{unexplained variance}}{\text{total variance}},$$

see *ibid.*, pp. 295–99.

[5] At least this is true if we think of "mistakes" as squared deviations from the true value.

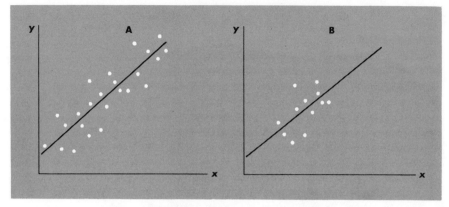

Figure 7–11   Regression and Correlation, with the Independent Variable Attenuated

CORRELATION AND REGRESSION COMPARED

Our discussion so far leaves us with the question, "Is correlation or regression analysis the better way to measure the strength of a relationship?" Obviously, the answer must be, "Sometimes one is, sometimes the other." The key to deciding when to use each measure lies in the fact that the correlation coefficient reflects the variability of the independent variable directly, whereas the regression coefficient does not.

Consider the two scattergrams in Figure 7–11. The scattergram from graph A has been reproduced in graph B, except that all observations for which the independent variable is less than 2 or greater than 4 have been cut out. The effect is to reduce the variability of the independent variable, while leaving the basic relationship between the independent and dependent variables unchanged. *Under these circumstances, the regression coefficient in B will be approximately the same as that in A, but the correlation coefficient will be sharply lowered in B.*

Let us see why this should be so. The regression line which minimized squared deviations in the full set of data in graph A should continue to minimize squared deviations in the partial set of data in graph B. Therefore, we would expect that the regression coefficient should be about the same in both graphs. On the other hand, because the variability of the independent variable has been reduced in graph B, so that it cannot shift very much in either direction, it cannot push the dependent variable very far. Relative to other causes of the dependent variable, which are just as free to vary as they were in graph A, the importance of the independent variable as a cause of the dependent variable must decline. But this is simply to say that the proportion of the total variance which is attributable to this independent variable declines. In other words, r^2 is reduced.

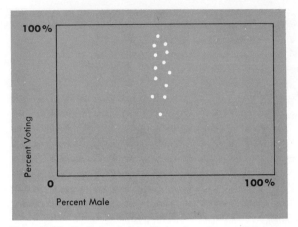

Figure 7–12   Predicting Percent Voting from Percent Male

This becomes a matter of considerable importance in field research, because generally the variability of independent variables is beyond the investigator's control. For instance, a researcher might be interested in knowing whether sex or race had more to do with whether a person voted. He might use census tract data on a large city, correlating percent black with percent voting and percent male with percent voting. But the distribution of people in most cities is such that the percent black would vary greatly while the percent male would not. (Blacks are concentrated highly in some tracts and almost absent in others; men are spread more or less evenly across all the tracts.)

The fact that percent male scarcely varies from one census tract to another guarantees that this researcher would find practically no correlation between percent male and percent voting. This is indicated in the hypothetical scattergram in Figure 7–12. Because there is near zero variance in percent male, very little of the variance in percent voting can be due to it. On the other hand, if residential patterns were such that percent male could vary as much as percent black does, it might be that sex would show up as a major determinant of voter turnout.[6] There is limited usefulness to a measure which would have us conclude from this that race is a more important cause of participation than sex.

[6] This example also incorporates a major statistical problem in some correlation and regression analysis, the so-called "ecological fallacy." This can occur when data on aggregate units (such as percent black, median income, and so on for census tracts, counties, or states) are used to infer how variables are related among individuals living in those aggregate units. See Robinson, 1950, and Stokes, 1969.

In a similar example, it frequently is asserted that academic departments should drop the Graduate Record Examination test scores as a factor in graduate admission. Among other—and better—reasons, this argument sometimes is based on the fact that in looking over the records of students in a department, it frequently turns out that how they did once they were admitted to the department is almost totally unrelated to their GRE scores. On the face of it, this is startling. But it ignores the fact that because GRE scores were an important factor in the department's choice of applicants, the variability of GRE scores for the students in the department is quite low. In other words, if the department cuts off applicants at the eightieth percentile, it should not expect its students' scores to be related to how they do in the department. By choosing them on that basis, it has insured that they all have virtually the same, or very close, scores. If the department stopped using the exam scores as a basis for admission and developed a graduate student body with a greater variance in scores, it would not necessarily still be true that scores would be unrelated to performance.

The problem with using correlation coefficients in either of these cases is that while the coefficient is affected by the particular variance of the independent variable in the data at hand, the investigator clearly intends to extrapolate from these particular data to a more general case. In the census tract study, he wants to make a statement about the impact of race or sex on voting, regardless of how people are located in the city. In the GRE study, he wants to make a judgment about how to treat new applicants (among whom the variability of GRE scores would be higher) on the basis of the relationship between GRE scores and grades among the students currently in the department.

A good rule is that in any situation in which you wish to extrapolate from a particular set of data to a more general case, you should use regression coefficients. Because theoretical research almost always is interested in generalizing, then, regression analysis usually will be superior to correlation analysis. (This advice holds in spite of the fact, which I mentioned earlier, that in regression analysis there is always some difficulty in handling varying units.)

There are circumstances, however, in which you may not intend to generalize, but only to describe a particular situation. For instance, someone might want to describe how a particular Congress, say the Eightieth or the Ninety-second, operated. It would then be appropriate to note that in that Congress, there was a negligible correlation between congressmen's race and their votes on various bills. This would help establish what were the important factors influencing outcomes *in that Congress*. Note, however, that this would not suggest that race still would be unrelated to votes when the time came that there was a significant number of blacks in Congress.

FURTHER DISCUSSION

In this chapter I have drawn only the broad outlines of correlation and regression analysis for interval data. In fact, I have purposely refrained from giving formulas for calculating these measures, so that anyone wishing to use the measures himself would be forced to go into them more thoroughly elsewhere. A good standard text in statistics for social scientists is Hubert M. Blalock, *Social Statistics* (1960); another is Allen L. Edwards, *Statistical Methods* (1967). William L. Hays' *Statistics* (1963) is an excellent text, which goes more thoroughly into the theory of statistics than Blalock or Edwards does.

One question you might consider is this: What would happen in a regression analysis if the independent variable did not vary at all? If, say, we wanted to relate voting turnout to education, but everyone in our study had the same amount of education? This question looks ahead to the material in Chapter 9.

INTRODUCTION TO STATISTICS
FURTHER TOPICS ON MEASUREMEMENT OF RELATIONSHIPS

8

In this chapter, I shall build on the introduction in Chapter 7 to discuss briefly the measurement of relationships among ordinal and nominal variables, the measurement of relationships which involve dichotomous variables, and the measurement of relationships which involve several variables simultaneously.*

	As we saw at the beginning of the preceding chapter, there are two main ways in which we can measure the strength of a relationship. We can measure how much change is produced in the dependent variable by a change in the independent variable, or we can measure how strongly the dependent variable is determined by the independent variable, relative to other things
MEASURES OF RELATIONSHIP FOR ORDINAL DATA	

which also help determine it.

Only for the second of these is it possible to develop a standard measure for use with ordinal- or nominal-scale data. In order to measure how much change is produced in the dependent variable, it is necessary to have some sort of unit in which to measure that change. But this is not available under ordinal or nominal measurement. Accordingly, the most we can hope for from ordinal or nominal variables is some form of correlational analysis.

A cross-tabulation is to the analysis of ordinal variables what a scattergram is to the analysis of interval variables. Consider Table 8–1. Like a scattergram, it shows how frequently various combinations of the two variables occur. (Each number in the table gives the number of northern whites in the study who exhibit a given combination of years of education and

* This chapter presents advanced material which can be skipped over without any loss in comprehension of the remaining material covered in this book.

Table 8–1   Relationship between Education and Attitude Toward Racial Integration, Using Northern Whites

Attitude Toward Integration	Education			
	Less than High School	High School	High School Plus	College Graduate
Favorable	90	80	108	88
So-so	162	119	135	40
Unfavorable	62	31	16	4

Source: 1968 Presidential Election Survey, University of Michigan (Survey Research Center Study SRC S523).

attitude toward integration; these are actual numbers of cases, not percentages.) The table shows a pattern to the relationship, just as a scattergram does, with attitudes favorable to integration occurring relatively more frequently as the level of education increases. (For instance, 88 out of 132 college graduates favor integration, compared to 80 out of 230 high school graduates.) The only differences between this table and a scattergram are:

(1) Because there is a limited number of values available for each variable, it is not necessary to use the infinite space of a plane to locate the observations. Instead, the observations are located in one or another of the cells of a table. Because so many observations are tied on these values, their presence is indicated by counting the number of observations falling in each cell and printing the number there, rather than by printing a dot for each observation. If the observations were indicated by dots, as in Figure 8–1, the similarity to a scattergram would become more obvious.

(2) Because there are no units in which to measure the difference between two values of a variable, however, the *precise* pattern in the table is meaningless. How great a change there is in attitudes as we move from "less than high school" to "high school" tells us practically nothing, because for all we know, "less than high school" might represent only slightly less education than "high school." [1]

Thus it is not possible to measure the strength of relationships in a way analogous to regression. On the other hand, it *is* possible to develop

[1] Of course, we probably know more than nothing about the differences between values in these variables. For instance, we know or can assume that "college graduate" means at least four more years of education than high school. There is more information here than we are allowed to use if we treat the variables as ordinal ones. This illustrates the argument made in Chapter 5 for "enriching" data measured at the ordinal or nominal level.

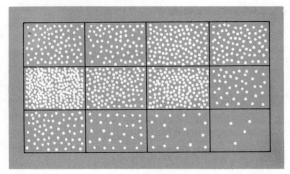

Figure 8–1

measures analogous to the correlation coefficient. All that is needed is to develop models of the perfect relationship and of perfect independence, as was done with the correlation coefficient, and a measure which indicates how close the data in a table come to these two models.

One such measure for use with ordinal variables, which is rather popular, is the Goodman and Kruskal Gamma.[2] It takes as its model of perfect independence a table in which the data are distributed uniformly throughout the table—that is, the same percent of each category of the dependent variable occurs at each category of the independent variable, and vice versa. Under such "perfect independence," the data in Table 8–1 would appear as in Table 8–2.

The model of a perfect positive relationship for the Gamma is one in which, when each observation is compared with each of the others, it is never true that when the first observation's value on one variable is *higher*

Table 8–2 "Independent" Version of Table 8–1

Attitude Toward Integration	Education			
	Less than High School	High School	High School Plus	College Graduate
Favorable	123	90	101	52
So-so	153	112	127	64
Unfavorable	38	28	31	16

[2] This measure is described in Goodman and Kruskal, 1954.

than the second observation's value on that variable, the first observation's value on the other variable is *lower* than the value of the second observation on that variable. For instance, in Table 8–1, a pair of observations in which one respondent favors integration and has less than high school education, but the other is "so-so" on integration and has a high school education, is inconsistent with a positive relationship between the two variables. The model of a perfect negative relationship for the Gamma is simply one in which it is always true that pairs of observations are inconsistent with a positive relationship.

In computing Gamma, each observation is compared with each other observation in this way. The number of such pairs which are inconsistent with a positive relationship is subtracted from the number which are consistent.[3] In Table 8–1, the figure is: $62 \times (80 + 108 + 88 + 119 + 135 + 40) + 162 \times (80 + 108 + 88) - 162 \times (31 + 16 + 4) - 90 \times (119 + 135 + 40 + 31 + 16 + 4) + 31 \times (108 + 88 + 135 + 40) + 119 \times (108 + 88) - 119 \times (16 + 4) - 80 \times (135 + 40 + 16 + 4) + 16 \times (88 + 40) + 135 \times (88) - 135 \times (4) - 108 \times (40 + 4) = 128,805$ consistent pairs $- 62,584$ inconsistent pairs $= 66,221$. That is, each of the 62 observations in the lower left-hand cell forms a positive pair with each of the 570 observations occurring above it and to the right. Each of the 162 observations in the second cell up on the left forms a positive pair with each of the 276 observations occurring above it and to the right and forms a negative pair with each of the 51 observations occurring below it and to the right. And so on.

The end figure, 66,221 in this case, is then divided by the total number of pairs which were compared $(128,805 + 62,584)$.[4] Accordingly, if all of the pairs formed were positive, Gamma would equal $+1$; if equal numbers of pairs were positive and negative (that is, if the data were distributed uniformly in the table, as in Table 8–2), Gamma would equal zero; if all of the pairs were negative, Gamma would equal -1. Like the correlation coefficient, therefore, Gamma ranges from -1 to $+1$, according to how nearly the data approximate a model of "perfect positive relationship." In the example from Table 8–1, Gamma equals $+.346$.

In Table 8–3, a few distributions of data which would yield Gamma's of $+1$ or -1 are depicted. Here "N" simply indicates that there is some number of observations falling in a cell; "O" indicates that the cell is empty.

One thing to remember in working with Gamma, as in working with

[3] Pairs of observations which share a common value on either of the two variables are ignored in this counting, inasmuch as such a pair can be neither consistent nor inconsistent with a positive relationship.

[4] Another popular measure, Kendall's Tau, is similar to Gamma. The numerators of the two measures are the same, and the denominator of Tau can be interpreted as an attempt to approximate the denominator of Gamma.

Table 8–3   Examples of Tables Producing Perfect Gamma's

Gamma $= +1$				Gamma $= +1$				Gamma $= -1$			
Hi	O O N N			Hi	O O O O			Hi	N O O O		
	O O N O				O O O N				N N O O		
	O O N O				O O N O				O O N O		
	O N O O				O N O O				O O O N		
Lo	N O O O			Lo	N O O O			Lo	O O O N		
	Lo Hi				Lo Hi				Lo Hi		

linear correlation, is that the Gamma measures only how closely the data approximate one particular model of a perfect relationship. For example, although the pattern of data in Table 8–4 looks like a very interesting distribution and is a "strong" U-shaped relationship, it would yield a very low Gamma, probably near zero. Many pairs of observations would be consistent with a positive relationship, and many others would be inconsistent with it.

Unlike the correlation coefficient, there is no way to develop a clear interpretation of what a shift of a given number of units in Gamma means, except that the further from zero Gamma is, the more nearly it approximates a perfect negative or positive relationship.

MEASURES OF RELATIONSHIP FOR NOMINAL DATA

In relating two nominally measured variables, the cross-tabulation still fills the main function of the scattergram. That is, it shows which values of one variable tend to coincide with which values of the other. But, in contrast to a table relating ordinal variables, the *position* of a cell in the table no longer tells us anything, for the order of values of a nominal variable means nothing. Consider the example in Table 8–5. Versions A and B of the table are equivalent; the table could not be rearranged in this way if the variables were measured ordinally.

As with ordinally measured data, all we can do in measuring the

Table 8–4   A Weak Gamma

Hi	O O O N N O				
	O O N O N O				
	O N O O O N				
Lo	N O O O O N				
	Lo Hi				

Table 8–5   Interchangeable Order in Nominal Data

Candidate Preferred	A Religion			Candidate Preferred	B Religion		
	Catholic	Protestant	Other		Protestant	Catholic	Other
X	20	0	0	Y	30	5	4
Y	5	30	4	Z	0	0	26
Z	0	0	26	X	0	20	0

strength of a relationship between two nominally measured variables is to assess the degree to which one variable is determined by the other. Probably the most useful measure available for this is the Goodman-Kruskal Tau-A.

Like the correlation coefficient and the Goodman-Kruskal Gamma, the Goodman-Kruskal Tau-A is set up in such a way that it takes on a value of +1.0 for "perfect" dependence and 0.0 for "perfect" independence. Because there is no pattern to a nominal-scale relationship, there can be no distinction between a positive and a negative relationship. Thus, Tau-A, like all nominal-scale measures, cannot take on negative values in the way that Gamma and the correlation coefficient do.

The models of "perfect" relationship and "perfect" lack of relationship used in working with nominal-scale variables must be based in one way or another on the extent to which certain values of one variable tend to cluster with certain values of the other variable. Because there is no pattern defined for the relationship, this is all there is to work with. Goodman and Kruskal have devised a useful and simple expression of such relationships, which has the advantage of having a clear interpretation at all values—an advantage which we noted was lacking in their Gamma and in the correlation coefficient if it was not squared.

They base their model of relationship on the idea that what one usually is interested in when one uses a relationship is predicting what value the dependent variable will have at given values of the independent variable. That is, if we are interested in knowing that there is a relationship between length of office in Congress and influence there, it is because we would like to pick out who the most influential congressmen should be. If we are interested in the relationship between class and voting, it is because we would like to develop a theory which will predict who is likely to vote Republican.

Table 8–6   Extreme Models of Relationship for Tau-A

A	Dem	Rep	Abst	Total
Catholic	80	0	0	80
Jewish	0	0	20	20
Protestant	0	100	0	100
Total	80	100	20	200

B	Dem	Rep	Abst	Total
Catholic	32	40	8	80
Jewish	8	10	2	20
Protestant	40	50	10	100
Total	80	100	20	200

A measure of the strength of a relationship should serve to tell us how accurately we will be able to make predictions by knowing about the relationship. It should measure how useful the relationship will be in making such predictions.

As the model of a perfect relationship, Goodman and Kruskal choose the situation in which, using our knowledge of a relationship, we could predict to the dependent variable without making any mistakes at all. As their model of perfect independence, they choose the situation in which, even knowing about the relationship and taking the independent variable into account, we would make as many mistakes as we would have made had we simply *guessed* what the dependent variable would be.

Table 8-6(A) illustrates a perfect relationship in this model. Under these circumstances, if we knew a person's religion, we could always predict his vote perfectly. Table 8–6(B) illustrates perfect independence. Working with these data we would make as many mistakes in trying to predict how people voted from their religion as we would make if we predicted "blind." For instance, in predicting blindly how a person voted, the best guess in both tables would be Republican, since more of the voters were Republican than any other single thing. If we guessed "Republican" each time, for the 200 cases, we would make a wrong guess 80 + 20 = 100 times. Now from Table 8–6(B), knowing people's religion would not improve our accuracy. If we guessed "Republican" (the best guess) for each of the Catholics, we would be wrong 32 + 8 = 40 times. In guessing similarly for the Jews we would be wrong 8 + 2 = 10 times, and for the Protestants, 40 + 10 = 50 times. Thus, in guessing each person's vote from his religion, we would be wrong 40 + 10 + 50 = 100 times—as often as in predicting blind.

For the data in Table 8-6(A), on the other hand, the best guess for a

Catholic would be "Democratic," and we would make no mistakes guessing that way. Similarly, we would make no mistakes guessing "abstained" for a Jew and "Republican" for a Protestant. Knowing an individual's religion would allow us to predict his vote perfectly.

The Goodman-Kruskal Tau-A shows where a particular relationship falls between these polar types. Where L is the number of mistakes one would make by predicting blindly, and M is the number of mistakes one would make by predicting on the basis of the independent variable,

$$\text{Tau-A} = \frac{L - M}{L}.$$

That is, Tau-A is the proportion by which one can reduce errors in predicting scores on the dependent variable by bringing in the independent variable as a prediction tool. In Table 8-6(A), for instance, Tau-A = (100 − 0)/100. One would make 100 mistakes predicting blindly, and one would make no mistakes predicting from religion; Tau-A equals 1.0. In Table 8–6(B), Tau-A = (100 − 100)/100. One would make no fewer mistakes by predicting from religion than by predicting blindly; the proportional reduction in errors in this case is 0.0. Though I have used the two extreme levels of a relationship in my example here, Tau-A retains this handy ability to be interpreted at all levels.

Although the Tau-A works out so nicely, it is by no means an ideal measure of relationship. Measures of relationship have been particularly difficult to work out for nominal-scale data, and there is quite a proliferation of them.[5] As an example of the problems one encounters in working with these measures, consider the following two disadvantages of the Tau-A.

(1) If the "best guess" is the same for each category of the independent variable, then Tau-A will always be zero, even though by most criteria we would say that there was a relationship between the variables. Table 8–7 gives an example of this. Let us take religion to be the independent variable in this table. Then the best guess for each category is Republican, and one would guess Republican each of the 550 times, *whether guessing blind or guessing on the basis of religion.* Obviously he would make the same mistakes in guessing each time. Thus, Tau-A equals:

$$\frac{(150 + 100) - (65 + 60 + 15 + 20 + 70 + 20)}{(150 + 100)}$$
$$= \frac{250 - 250}{250} = 0.$$

[5] For a few of these see Goodman and Kruskal, *op. cit.,* and Siegel, 1956.

Table 8-7   An Awkward Situation for Tau-A

	Dem	Rep	Abst	Total
Catholic	65	70	60	195
Jewish	15	30	20	65
Protestant	70	200	20	290
Total	150	300	100	550

But the percent-Republican ranges from 35.9 percent for Catholics and 46.1 percent for Jews to 66.7 percent for the Protestants. By almost any standard but the Tau-A, religion has a considerable impact on how these people vote.

(2) Whenever there are fewer categories in the independent variable than there are in the dependent variable, it is impossible for Tau-A to reach a value of 1.0. Table 8-8 furnishes an example of this. Here, the data from Table 8-6(A) have been collapsed into a two-by-three table by combining Catholics and Jews into "non-Protestants." Although these are the same data which indicated a perfect relationship in a three-by-three table, they cannot do so now. If there are more categories in the dependent variable than in the independent variable, then at least one category of the independent variable must involve multiple categories of the dependent variable. (As "non-Protestant" involves "Democratic" and "abstention" in this example.) If this is so, then predicting on the basis of the independent variable cannot eliminate all of the errors which would be made predicting blindly. In this example

$$\text{Tau-A} = \frac{(80 + 20) - (0 + 20 + 0 + 0)}{(80 + 20)}$$

Table 8-8   Another Awkward Situation for Tau-A

	Dem	Rep	Abst	
Non-Protestant	80	0	20	100
Protestant	0	100	0	100
Total	80	100	20	

$$= \frac{100 - 20}{100} = \frac{80}{100} = .8.$$

I have cited these disadvantages of the Tau-A not to discredit it as a measure. I personally prefer it to any other measure yet developed for working with nominal-scale variables. If the best such measure involves problems like the two I have discussed, this should convince you to always pay close attention to exactly what is going on in a table. It might be that one measure is not suitable for a particular problem and that you should consider an alternative measure. It might even be that the most interesting thing going on in a table would be lost in any summary measure. For instance, in Table 8–7 it is possible that what would be most interesting is not the overall dependence between religion and voting, but the particularly low abstention rate among Protestants. This is a point to which I shall return in concluding this chapter.

A NOTE ON DICHOTOMIES

Dichotomies are classifications which involve only two categories. For example, sex: male and female; race: white and nonwhite; referendum vote: yes and no; participation: voter and nonvoter. Such classifications have a useful property, which is a bit mysterious: although they are nominal scales, they can quite properly be treated as if they were interval scales and can be analyzed using measures appropriate for interval scales.

The trick—of course, it is not really a trick—is this. Because such a variable can take on only two values, there is a common unit in which the difference between values of the variable from one observation to the next can be measured. This unit is simply the difference between the two categories. Let us call the categories A and B. Then the distance between two observations having category A is zero units, the distance between two observations having category B is zero units, and the distance between two observations, one of which has A and the other B, is one unit. Because there usually is no natural ordering to the dichotomy, the decision of whether A is one unit greater than B, or one unit less, must be an arbitrary one.

An alternative way of looking at what is going on is to think of a dichotomy as measuring the degree to which an observation embodies one of its categories. The category is either present or not present for each observation. For instance, the dichotomy "sex: male and female," also can be looked at as a variable "femaleness" (or alternatively, "maleness"; the choice is arbitrary). Each subject is either totally "female" or totally not "female." If the difference between totally female and not female at all is taken to be one unit, then women have values of $+1.0$ for the variable "femaleness" and

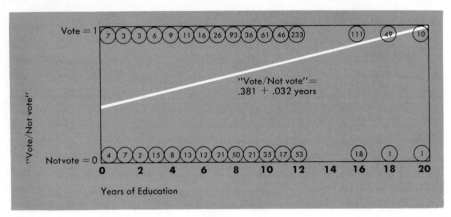

Figure 8–2 Relationship Between Years of Education and Dichotomous Variable "Vote/Not-Vote."

Source: SRC 1968 American National Election Study (SRC 45523).

men have values of 0.0. This is a true interval measure, and can be used together with other interval measures, such as income or age, in regression and correlation analysis.

The same interpretation cannot be placed on nominal-scale variables with more than two categories. We would have no common unit, for example, in which to place Catholics relative to Protestants or Jews in the variable "religion."

Figure 8–2 presents an example of regression analysis using a dichotomous dependent variable. The circled numbers show the number of dots which fall at each point in the scattergram relating the two values. (There are 53 individuals with twelve years of education and a score of zero on "vote/not-vote," for instance, and 233 individuals with twelve years of education and a score of one on "vote/not-vote.")

The regression line plotted through the dots shows that the average "vote/not-vote" score can be expected to rise by .032 with each additional year of education. There is a particularly useful interpretation of the regression line when the dependent variable is a dichotomy. The "average value" of a dichotomous variable is actually the proportion of individuals having a score of one on the dichotomy. If six out of ten individuals have a score of one on such a variable, for instance, the average score of the ten individuals is:

$$\frac{1 + 1 + 1 + 1 + 1 + 1 + 0 + 0 + 0 + 0}{10} = \frac{6}{10} = .6.$$

Thus, when the regression line tells us that we may expect those with eleven years of education to have an average score on "vote/not-vote" of .381 + (.032 × 11), or .733, this means the same thing as saying that we may expect 73.3 percent of those with eleven years of education to vote.

It might be tempting, when faced with the difficulties of working with nominally or ordinarily measured variables, to cut the Gordian knot by collapsing these variables into dichotomies and treating them as interval variables. "Religion," for instance, might be collapsed into "Protestant/non-Protestant." This backward analog of the "enrichment" of measurement which I suggested in Chapter V is only very rarely either useful or necessary, however. It should be intuitively clear that its effects generally would be pernicious, simply because it involves throwing away information. And fortunately, it is hardly ever necessary. Used in multivariate analysis (which I cannot treat in any detail in this book, but which I shall touch on in the next section), a variable with several categories can be treated as a series of dichotomies and included in regression or correlation analysis in this way. For instance, "religion" can be translated into a *group* of dichotomous variables: "Presbyterian/non-Presbyterian," "Methodist/non-Methodist," "Catholic/non-Catholic," and so on. Each individual presumably would have a score of one on one of these and scores of zero on the others. This whole group of dichotomous variables can then be included together in a multivariate regression analysis. Variables such as these generally are known as "dummy variables," or "binary variables."

MULTIVARIATE ANALYSIS

In Chapter 6, we saw that frequently it is important to hold one variable constant while measuring the relationship between two other variables. The easiest way to do this is literally to "hold the variable constant," as in the example on page 100, by separating the subjects into groups along the control variable. (A group of Democrats, a group of Republicans, and a group of independents, for example, if registration is the variable to be held constant.) The relationship between the other two variables is then measured for each group.

This technique has important disadvantages. First, if we want to control for an intervally measured variable, the number of "groups" we set up might be too large. For instance, in controlling for income, we might have a group of all those with an income of $8,243, another of all those with an income of $23,402, and so on; in this case there probably would be as many groups as there were subjects in the study. This problem can be averted by lumping subjects into a few broad categories of the independent variable, but doing so throws away a great deal of the precision in the measure—something one may not want to do.

A second, and more serious, problem in literally holding a variable constant is that the process quite rapidly leaves the researcher with only small numbers of subjects among whom to measure a relationship. Suppose he wanted to look at the relationship between occupation and voting, holding constant race and age. He might then divide the population into groups such as blacks aged twenty to thirty, whites aged twenty to thirty, blacks aged thirty-one to forty, and so on, and then look at the occupation/vote relationship for each of these groups. But the typical national survey, with about two thousand respondents, might include no more than five or six whites aged twenty to thirty, blacks aged fifty-one to sixty, or whatever. Such small groups would give very unreliable estimates of the relationship between occupation and vote.[6]

A final disadvantage of literal controlling is that it produces a series of measures of the relationship (one measure for each group) which is unwieldy and difficult to absorb. Particularly if we wanted to control simultaneously for more than one variable, as in the example of race and age above, this might leave us with as many as twenty or thirty separate measures to consider.

Fortunately, there is an easier way to control for a variable, or at least there is an easier way if we are using interval-scale variables. The technique of multivariate regression allows us to look at the pattern in several variables among all of our observations (without breaking these down into separate subgroups) and to estimate what the relationship between the dependent variable and any particular independent variable would be if none of the other variables varied—that is, if each of the other variables were "held constant."

It is beyond the scope of this book to go into any detail on the technique, but I will sketch it out in the most general way, using as an example the case of two independent variables (w and x) and a dependent variable (y).

You will recall that the relationship between two variables can be plotted in a flat space of two dimensions (represented by a scattergram). Similarly, the relationship among three variables can be plotted in a three-dimensional space, as seen in Figure 8–3. The vertical dimension is the dependent variable, and each of the horizontal dimensions is one of the independent variables. Each observation is a dot floating in the three-dimensional space, located according to its values on each of the three variables. Dot "A" has had coordinates drawn to show how it is located in the three-dimensional space by its values on w, x, and y, where these values are p, q, and r, respectively.

Just as a one-dimensional line through the two-dimensional scattergram could summarize the pattern in a two-variable relationship, so a two-dimensional plane through the three-dimensional scattergram can summarize

---

[6] See the discussion of the Law of Large Numbers above, p. 64.

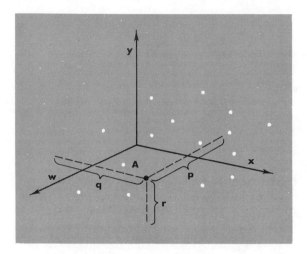

Figure 8–3 A Three-Dimensional Scattergram

the pattern in its three-variable relationship. The plane is picked on the basis of the same criterion by which the regression line was chosen. It must be the plane that minimizes the sum of squared deviations of actual y values from the y values predicted from the plane.

This regression plane would look like a flat piece of cardboard set at some tilt in the middle of the three-dimensional space, over a grid containing all possible combinations of values of w and x. By counting out a certain distance along x and then a certain distance along w, we can locate a particular combination of w and x on this grid. The height of the cardboard plane above the grid at this point is the value of y predicted from the given values of w and x by the regression plane. The regression equation associated with the plane is of the form:

$$y = a + b_1w + b_2x$$

As in the two variable case, a is the intercept—the predicted value of y when both x and w equal zero. Similarly, b_1 tells by how many units y can be expected to increase if w increases by one unit *and x does not change;* and b_2 tells by how many units y can be expected to increase if x increases by one unit *and w does not change.* Here b_1 and b_2 are the regression coefficients of the equation.

To calculate from the multivariate regression equation the y value which you would expect from a particular combination of w and x, you:

1.   Start with a, the expected value of y when both x and w equal zero.

2.   Add to this b_1 times w, or the amount by which y could be expected to change if the value of w shifted from zero to the particular value you are using. At this point, you have the expected value of y, if x equals zero and w equals the particular value.

3.   To this sum, add b_2 times x, the amount by which y could be expected to change if x shifted from zero to the particular value you are using, and w remained unchanged. You now have the expected value of y, given these particular values of w and x.

Notice in this that b_1 describes the relationship between w and y if x is held constant, and that b_2 describes the relationship between x and y if w is held constant. In this way, without requiring us to break our observations into separate small and awkward groups, multivariate regression allows us to examine relationships with certain other variables controlled.

For example, if we had data for United States counties giving the percent black students in the county attending all-black schools, the median income of the county, and the percent black in the county population, we might find the following situation:

Let I be the percent of black students attending all-black schools.
Let M be the county's median income (in thousands of dollars).
Let B be the percent black in the county's population.

On examining the relationship between I and M, we might find that the regression equation was:

$$I = 68.2 - 10.1 \ M$$

This would indicate that integration of schools is greater in richer counties. The percent of blacks attending all-black schools decreases by 10.1 percent as the median income of the county increases by a thousand dollars.

But it obviously is necessary to control for percent black in measuring this relationship. It might be that the apparent integration of the well-heeled counties is simply a result of the fact that in the richer counties there are so few blacks that it is difficult to find enough of them to fill an all-black school. We could test for this by adding the variable "percent black" as an additional independent variable. The regression equation:

$$I = 49.5 - 1.3 \ M + .6 \ B$$

would indicate that this is true. With the control for "percent black" added, the relationship between median income and percent of black students attending all-black schools largely disappears. In the multiple regression equation, a decrease of only 1.3 percent can be expected from an increase of a thousand dollars in median income.[7]

This freedom from the need to "hold variables constant" physically is an important advantage of multivariate regression analysis. This is especially true when one is working with several variables simultaneously.[8] There is no satisfactory analog to this technique for working with ordinal data. This is another argument, which I could not make at the time in Chapter 5, for trying to measure variables intervally as often as possible. Nominal variables may be included in multiple regression equations by treating them as "dummy variables."[9]

As in simple linear regression, it is important in multiple linear regression that the data actually fit a model in which all the relationships between the dependent variable and the independent variables are linear. Otherwise, the regression plane described by the equation we come up with will be an inaccurate representation of the relationships.

There is also an additional requirement in *multiple* linear regression. It is important that the data best fit a model in which the relationship between the dependent variable and each independent variable is the same, no matter what value the other independent variable(s) takes on. In the above example of w, x, and y, we had to assume that an increase of a unit in x produced the same change in y, no matter what the value of w was. Otherwise, we could not have calculated the expected value of y by simply adding a and b_1 times w and b_2 times x. We would have had to pick a value for b_1 which was appropriate for whatever value of x we were using, and a value of b_2 which was appropriate for whatever value of w we were using. It is obvious that this would be a complicated procedure. In fact, it is often impossible to operate under these conditions.

When this happens—when the relationship between variables A and B differs, depending on the value of a variable C—there is said to be "interaction" among the variables. A concrete example may make more clear what "interaction" is, and how it might arise. Consider the relationship between congressmen's party affiliation and their vote on a bill. This relationship could be strong (all Democrats vote one way, all Republicans the other), or weak (less clear-cut party differences). Now, the strength of the relationship might be related to congressmen's seniority. New congressmen, who

---

[7] This little analysis is wholly fictitious. For a multiple regression analysis of black voting registration, using county data for the southern states, see Matthews and Prothro, 1963.

[8] Although I have used the case of three variables in this section because that case can be represented by perspective drawings, the general multivariate regression technique applies to any number of variables. The same logic would apply to a four variable case, with an equation: $y = a + b_1w + b_2x + b_3z$, although no scattergram can be drawn in these four dimensions.

[9] See above, p. 137.

Interaction in Research and Theory

Although interaction among variables is a nuisance from the standpoint of multivariate regression analysis, it is itself an interesting type of relationship. It is exciting to think that a relationship itself may depend on a further variable. Because interaction occurs with some frequency among social science variables, it is important that you be alert to it in your research. Because "common sense" rarely gets so complicated as to suggest this sort of thing, interaction is almost always unexpected, and discovering it is fun and dramatic. As one example, Philip Converse was able to argue very neatly for the importance of a measure of ideological sophistication by showing that the relationship between social class and voting was strongly affected by it.[11] Among men who scored lowest in ideological sophistication, there was no relationship between social class and voting. As the score on ideological sophistication increased, a relationship between class and vote appeared, reaching its highest strength among men with the highest sophistication score.

are very dependent on their party leadership for favors, might vote obediently along straight party lines. More senior congressmen, who had built up positions of strength for themselves, might vote more independently.

Thus, there would be interaction among the variables. The relationship between party and vote would change as the third variable, seniority, changed. Under these circumstances, a regression equation of the form:

$$\text{Vote} = a + b_1\text{Party} + b_2\text{Seniority}$$

would not be appropriate. It would not be true that "vote" increased by the same amount with a given change in "party." How much "vote" changed with a given change in "party" would depend on the value of "seniority."[10]

CONCLUSION	You might expect me to conclude now, "Go out and use these measures." But I am more interested in conditioning you against using them unwisely.

All of these techniques simplify what is going on in a set of data by screening out certain aspects of relationships. This is

---

[10] It is possible to add "interaction terms" to the regression equation to take into account certain types of interaction, but that goes beyond the scope of this presentation. See, for example, Blalock, 1969, Appendix A, "Theory Building and the Statistical Concept of Interaction."

[11] Converse, 1964, esp. pp. 231–34. This example is a particularly interesting one, because Converse demonstrates yet a second level of interaction (the interaction itself varies with sex) which I have not discussed above.

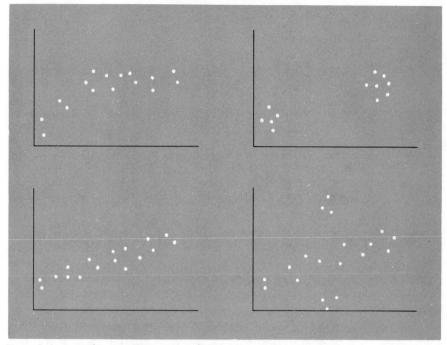

Figure 8–4   Four Alternative Scattergrams with the Same Regression Equation

their great virtue, and it *is* a virtue. But it is your responsibility to look and see at the same time just what is being screened out. For instance, each of the scattergrams in Figure 8–4 would give approximately the same regression equation, but the relationships depicted mean quite different things.

It is critical that you examine as carefully as possible each scattergram on which you base a regression equation, checking for nonlinearity, noting which observations are mavericks in the relationship, and so on. And you should look just as carefully at the table for which you calculate a Goodman-Kruskal Gamma or Tau-A. Look, for example, to see whether a particular cell of the table is out of line with the relationship in the rest of the cells, or which categories of the variable contribute most to the strength of the relationship.

A computer can chug out hundreds of Gammas in a few seconds. It is tempting simply to call for a mound of printout, especially given the uncertainty involved in working with most social science theories. But you usually will be better served if you first think carefully about what you want to do, pick a limited number of relationships you want to look at, and examine each of these relationships in detail. Your measures then will be useful summarizing tools, not substitutes for a full look at what is going on.

Data will talk to you, but you must let them speak softly.

INTRODUCTION TO STATISTICS
INFERENCE, OR HOW TO GAMBLE ON YOUR RESEARCH

9

As I pointed out in Chapter 7, there are two main areas of statistics: (1) measuring things, especially measuring relationships between variables; and (2) estimating how likely it is that the measure you have gotten could have occurred by chance. In Chapters 7 and 8 we looked at the first of these. In this chapter we shall look at the second. (I must note here that I am not going to teach you in this chapter *how to use* statistical tests. Instead, I shall present the general logic of such tests, to help you understand what they mean when you come across them. This also should serve as a useful supplement to a statistics course, which sometimes teaches students how to use the tests without putting the tests in a broader perspective.)

It is quite possible to get a particular result by chance, even though the result is not true in general. If you chose ten senators at random, for instance, it would not be difficult to come up with a group consisting largely of conservative Democrats and liberal Republicans. From that you might conclude—erroneously—that there was a relationship between party and ideology in the Senate, with Republicans being the more liberal group.

If you repeatedly drew groups of ten senators, selecting the ten at random from the whole Senate, *most* of the time you would find that the Democrats in your group were more liberal than the Republicans, simply because Democratic senators do tend to be somewhat more liberal than Republican senators. But some of the time, you would find that the Republicans in your group were more liberal than the Democrats, or that the two parties did not differ at all. The problem in drawing a single group and describing the Senate from it is that you cannot know whether your group is of the first type (the relationship between the variables is the same in your subset as in the Senate as a whole) or of the second (the relationship between the variables is different in the subset than in the Senate as a whole). If it is of the first type, a description of the Senate based on the group will be true; if it is of the second, the description of the Senate will be false. This is a general problem which must be dealt with whenever anyone tries to describe a whole population of cases by looking only at a sample drawn out of the population. It comes up in social science research, opinion polling, assigning television ratings, conducting market analyses, administering quality control in manufacturing, and numerous other places.

Fortunately, there are ways to figure out just how likely it is that a particular result could have occurred by chance, even if its opposite were generally true. There exist techniques by which we can calculate the odds that an opposite conclusion is really the true one and that our conclusion is, accordingly, false. That is, we can calculate how much stock to put in our findings. It is a very close analogy to say that we can gamble intelligently on the results of our study by calculating the odds that the results are false. When we do this, we are said to measure (or "test") the *statistical signifi-cance* of our results.

In looking at how to measure relationships in the previous chapter, we found that there were qualitatively different ways to go about it, depending on the level at which the variables were measured. In measuring the statis-tical significance of a relationship, one broad procedure holds for all levels of data, although there are differences in specific techniques.

THE LOGIC OF MEASURING SIGNIFICANCE

The general procedure by which we calculate the probability that a given result could have occurred by chance, even though the true state of affairs was something other than what is indicated by the re-sult, is the same procedure that we use in calculat-ing the "odds" of any event happening.

As usual when talking about probability, let us start with a deck of cards. Given an honest deck of cards, thoroughly shuffled, you are in-structed to draw a card. You know that the probability that you will draw the king of hearts is 1/52, for there are fifty-two cards and only one of them is the king of hearts. Next, you are instructed to do this two times, replacing the card and reshuffling after the first draw. You know that the probability of drawing a king of hearts *both times* is $1/52 \times 1/52 = 1/2704$; and so on.[1]

You were able to calculate these probabilities because, given a suffi-

---

[1] The logic of this is as follows: In order to draw two kings of hearts in two draws, one must accomplish two things. First, he must draw the king of hearts on the first round. He can expect this to happen only one fifty-second of the time. Finally, if he has drawn the king of hearts on the first round, he must draw it again on the second. Assuming that he has succeeded in the first round, he still can expect success in the second round only one fifty-second of the time. In other words, in the full two-draw process, he can expect to proceed to final success only one fifty-second of one fifty-second of the time.

cient set of assumptions, the probability that any particular result would occur could be determined. These assumptions had to account for all of the factors which could influence the outcome of the drawing. With such a set of assumptions, it was possible to calculate exactly how likely any particular result was. The set of assumptions in this case was:

1. the deck has fifty-two cards, of which only one is the king of hearts;
2. the deck is thoroughly and honestly shuffled before each drawing;
3. the drawing is blind, so that each card is equally likely to be drawn. (You don't peek, none of the cards stick together, and so on.)

If any of these assumptions were not true, then your calculation of probabilities would be incorrect. For instance, if there were two kings of hearts (i.e., assumption 1 was wrong), the probability of drawing one in a single draw would have been 2/52, not 1/52. Or, if the deck had been stacked so as to make drawing the king of hearts likely (i.e., assumption 2 was wrong), the probability of drawing one would have been greater than 1/52.

This is an example of the way in which we normally use odds and probability. We have a set of assumptions, of which we are confident. Those assumptions determine the probability that any particular event will happen. From this we know with how much confidence we can predict that the event will occur—that is, at what odds we should bet that it will occur.

Statistical inference uses this same logical structure, but turns it on its head. An example may be the best way to demonstrate this.

AN EXAMPLE OF STATISTICAL INFERENCE

Let us consider once more the example I used above, taking a sample of ten senators to see whether there is a difference in how liberal the two senatorial parties are. Let us say that you have drawn such a sample and that your results are shown in Table 9–1. Of the ten senators in the sample, the Democrats are more liberal than the Republicans. Seventy-five percent of the former, but only 33 percent of the latter, are liberal. But how safe would you be

Table 9–1   Sample Result

	Democrats	Republicans
Liberal	3	2
Conservative	1	4

in making such a statement about the Senate as a whole, based on just these ten senators?

To find out, you must start out just as you did in the card-drawing problem above, by setting a list of assumptions which are sufficient to let you calculate the probability of drawing ten senators that look like those you have, if in fact Democratic and Republic senators do not differ in the degree to which they are liberal. These assumptions are:

1. the ten senators have been drawn at random;
2. there is *no relationship* between party and ideology in the "full" Senate from which these have been drawn.

Just from these two assumptions, using probability theory, it is possible for you to calculate how likely it is that you would have gotten any particular result in your sample. In this particular case, using a "chi square" test (which I shall introduce later in this chapter), you can calculate that the probability of having gotten at least as great a difference as you found between the parties, given the assumptions, is .264.[2] Thus, there is a good chance that you could have gotten a relationship as strong as this in a sample of ten, even if the assumptions you have set up were true—that is, even if there were no difference between Democrats and Republicans.

How you would then treat your research results depends on whether you are a long-shot gambler at heart, what kind of risks ride on your decision, and so on. Approximately three times out of four you would not have gotten as strong a relationship as you did, if your assumptions were true. Will you reject that set of assumptions on the basis of your sample result, accepting the one chance in four that you are wrong in doing so? If you are willing to reject the assumptions, then notice that the truth is questionable with regard to only one of the assumptions in the set; you purposely have set up the test this way. You know whether or not you have drawn the ten senators at random. Therefore, in rejecting the set of assumptions, you really are rejecting only one assumption, the assumption that there is no relationship between party and ideology in the Senate. What you are saying is: "By rejecting its opposite, I am making the statement, 'There is an ideological difference between the Senatorial parties.' I know that, given the amount of evidence I have gathered, I am running considerable risk in making the statement. There is a probability of .264 that I am wrong."

---

[2] There is a great variety of statistical tests available to fit different circumstances of research. Statistical tests vary in the level of measurement that they require and in the particular set of assumptions that they embody. The "chi-square" test used here is particularly designed for testing the significance of a relationship between two nominal-scale variables. See below, pp. 150–53.

	The above example is a typical problem in statisti-
HYPOTHESIS-TESTING	cal inference. We have a particular result in hand.

The above example is a typical problem in statistical inference. We have a particular result in hand. We wish to calculate the probability that this event could have occurred, given some set of assumptions. We *cannot* be confident of these assumptions, for they involve the very things we are trying to infer. If there is a sufficiently *small* probability that the event we have in mind could have occurred, given the set of assumptions, we decide to treat the set of assumptions as false. (This usually is referred to as "rejecting the hypothesis" that the assumptions are true.)

We run some risk of being wrong in treating the assumptions as false. After all, the result we have observed *could* have occurred even if the assumptions were true. The probability that we have calculated tells us precisely how likely it is that we are wrong. It tells us the probability that the result we have observed could have occurred, if the assumptions we are rejecting were in fact true—that is, the probability that we are making a mistake in rejecting the assumptions. We normally will reject a set of assumptions only when the probability that they could have produced the result we have observed is comfortably low.[3]

You can see now why I said above that statistical inference uses the same logic as odds-setting, but turns it on its head. In everyday odds-setting, we use a set of assumptions which we are willing to accept in order to predict how likely it is that certain things will happen in the future. In statistical inference, we calculate how likely it is that a result, which we have observed, could have occurred if a set of assumptions, which we cannot observe directly, were true. If the probability is sufficiently low, we use the result to reject the assumptions; just as in everyday setting of odds, the probability shows us how likely it is that we are making a mistake.

THE NULL HYPOTHESIS

It is clear from the description of statistical inference above that we do not test directly the statement we wish to make about a relationship. Instead, we insert its opposite—which is called the "null hypothesis," the hypothesis we

---

[3] Whether the probability is "comfortably low," of course, is a difficult thing to judge. In odds-making, one usually has objective outside criteria to help in the decision—an amount of money to be lost if he is wrong, for instance. In much *engineering* research, there also will be such criteria available. In *theory-oriented* research, however, there usually are no criteria, because the result is supposed to hold, not just for some particular occasion, but in general. It is supposed to apply to occasions as yet unforeseen. Therefore, because objective criteria are lacking, a convention usually is followed of rejecting a set of assumptions only if the probability is less than .05.

should like to reject—into the set of assumptions from which we calculate the probability. Because it is the only questionable member of the set of assumptions, if we decide to reject the set we really are rejecting only the null hypothesis. By rejecting the null hypothesis we in effect assert its opposite, which is the statement we wished to make in the first place.

The twisted and convoluted way in which one must think in order to understand this is discouraging to most people when they see it for the first time. "Why," they ask, "can't we just test directly the statement we want to make, instead of having to think inside-out the way you do in statistical inference?"

But think about how you might do that. First of all, you could never test the hypothesis that your sample result was exactly the same as the true value in the population from which you had drawn the sample. Taken to a sufficient number of decimal places, it would virtually always *not* be the same as the true population value. For instance, 13.57993 percent of voters in the United States voted for George Wallace in 1968; no sample would have produced exactly this figure. But you would not want to conclude that you always had to reject every sample result.

Accordingly you would pick some range of values around the true value and test whether or not the sample result was in that range. But because you do not know what the true value is, this is a test which is impossible to set up.

In using the null hypothesis, on the other hand, a single alternative is chosen, which negates *all* possible true values which would be consistent with the statement you wish to make. For instance, in the Senate example, if you wanted to assert that your sample result was sufficiently close to the true relationship for you to accept the sample result as valid, you would have to choose among an infinite variety of possible true relationships (80 percent of Democrats liberal, 75 percent of Republicans liberal; 100 percent of Democrats liberal, 51 percent of Republicans liberal; 100 percent of Democrats liberal, 1 percent of Republicans liberal; and so on). By using a null hypothesis ("there is no difference between the parties"), you can deal with a single statement that negates all possible versions of the statement you want to make. It is simply easier to disprove a specific hypothesis than to prove an open-ended hypothesis.

AN EXAMPLE: χ^2

One popular significance test is χ^2 (chi-square), which was used in the example above. It is designed for use with a table relating two nominal-scale variables. Given the strength of the relationship between the variables in the table, χ^2 allows us to estimate the probability that there is no relationship between the variables in the full population from which the sample represented in the table has been drawn.

In Table 9–2, a hypothetical relationship between ethnicity and policy

Table 9–2 **Ethnicity and Preferred Government Action Priorities**

Preferred Priority	Ethnicity			
	WASP	Black	Other	Total
Employment & Welfare	30	27	53	110
Foreign Affairs	11	5	14	30
Environment	29	8	23	60
Total	70	40	90	200

priorities has been drawn, based on a sample of two hundred respondents to a survey. We want to know whether it is safe to assert, on the evidence of this sample, that there is a relationship between the two variables.

In order to calculate χ^2, this table must be compared with a construct of what it would look like if there were no relationship between the variables. Such a construct is shown in Table 9–3. The entries in Table 9–3 are arrived at by calculating how many WASPs, say, would give first priority to employment and welfare, if exactly the same proportion of WASPs as of blacks and "other ethnics" favored the employment/welfare priority. Thus, because there are 70 WASPs in the sample, and 110/200 of the sample favor the employment/welfare priority, we would expect to find that the sample contained 110/200 times 70, or 38.5 WASPs who chose employment/welfare. Similarly, we would expect to find that 110/200 of the 40 blacks, or 22.0 chose employment/welfare. And so on, cell by cell, until the hypothetical table was filled. Notice that in order to construct a table in which the variables are completely unrelated, it was necessary to maintain the fiction that there could have been one-half of a WASP in favor of the employment/welfare priority.

Table 9–3 embodies the null hypothesis which we want to test—that

Table 9–3   Table of Nonrelationship

Preferred Priority	Ethnicity			
	WASP	Black	Other	Total
Employment & Welfare	38.5	22.0	49.5	110
Foreign Affairs	10.5	6.0	13.5	30
Environment	21.0	12.0	27.0	60
Total	70	40	90	200

there is no relationship between the variables. Each cell in the table has the characteristic (a) that its entry is the same proportion of its row frequency as its column frequency is of the total sample, and (b) that its entry is the same proportion of its column frequency as its row frequency is of the total sample. That is, the members of each row are equally likely to fall into any given column, and vice versa. This is what we should expect if the two variables were unrelated.

The question we want to ask is: "Are the two tables sufficiently different that we can say, on the basis of our sample result, that the full population does not look like the distribution in the hypothetical table?" Chi-square is a measure of how different the two tables are. It can be calculated from the formula:

$$\chi^2 = \Sigma \, \frac{(F_o - F_h)^2}{F_h},$$

where for each cell in the table,

F_o = the observed frequency,

and

F_h = the predicted frequency for the hypothetical table.

Thus, for each cell in the table, (1) the prediction from the hypothetical table is subtracted from the actual figure; (2) this figure is squared; and (3) the squared difference is then divided by the prediction from the hypothetical table. The results of this, from all the cells of the table, are added together (you will recall that this is what the sign "Σ" means) to give us the x^2. The more the tables differ, the greater x^2 will be. If the tables are exactly the same, then x^2 will equal zero, inasmuch as each cell's result will be:

$$\frac{(F_o - F_h)^2}{F_h} = \frac{0^2}{F_h} = 0$$

in Table 9–4, x^2 is calculated for the present example. Cell "a" is the upper left-hand cell of Table 9–2 or 9–3 (the cell in which WASPS choosing employment/welfare fall), cell "b" is the next cell to the right, cell "c" is the upper right-hand cell, cell "d" is the middle left-hand cell, cell "e" falls at the exact center of the table, and so on.

SAMPLING DISTRIBUTIONS

Before I can show how we go from measuring the difference between the observed and null hypothesis tables to calculating the probability that the null hypothesis is true, I must first introduce the idea of a *sampling distribution*.

A sampling distribution shows, for any particular set of assumptions, what proportion of the time each particular result could be expected to occur, if the sampling technique you have used were repeated a very large number of times and the set of assumptions (including the null hypothesis) were true. That is, it gives the *probability* of getting any particular result, if you

Table 9–4   Calculations for x^2

Cell	F_h	$(F_o - F_h)$	$(F_o - F_h)^2$	$(F_o - F_h)^2/F_h$
a	38.5	−8.5	72.25	1.877
b	22.0	+5.0	25.00	1.136
c	49.5	+3.5	12.25	.247
d	10.5	+0.5	0.25	.024
e	6.0	−1.0	1.00	.167
f	13.5	+0.5	0.25	.019
g	21.0	+8.0	64.00	3.048
h	12.0	−4.0	16.00	1.333
i	27.0	−4.0	16.00	.593
			$x^2 =$ Total $=$	8.444

applied the techniques you are using to a population for which the null hypothesis was true.

A sampling distribution embodies all the assumptions you make in a test, including the null hypothesis. It represents the application of probability theory to those assumptions, to calculate the probability that each possible result would occur.

Some simple sampling distributions can be calculated easily. For instance, in the example on page 146, in which you were asked to figure the odds that the card you drew would be the king of hearts, the sampling distribution states that the probability of drawing the ace of hearts is 1/52, the probability of drawing the king of hearts is 1/52, and so on through all the cards of the deck. This sampling distribution depends on the set of assumptions which you made in that example. The sampling distribution for a different set of assumptions would look different.

In another simple case, suppose you had to predict the probability of getting just one head in two flips of a coin. Assume that: (1) the coin is honest, (2) the flipper is honest, and (3) the coin will not stand on its edge. You can now calculate that the probability of getting a head followed by a tail is 0.25, the probability of getting a head followed by a head is 0.25, the probability of getting a tail followed by a head is 0.25, and the probability of getting a tail followed by a tail is 0.25. Because two of the possibilities involve getting just one head in the two throws, the probability of getting just one head in either of the two ways is 0.50, the probability of getting no heads is 0.25, and the probability of getting two heads is 0.25. This sampling distribution is presented graphically in Figure 9–1.

The same sampling distribution could be presented in a cumulative graph, showing the probability of getting *at least* no heads, at least one head,

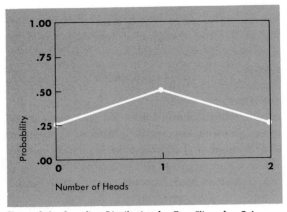

Figure 9–1   Sampling Distribution for Two Flips of a Coin

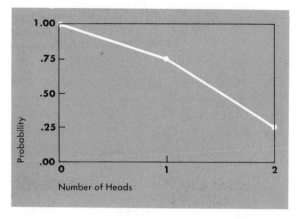

Figure 9–2   Cumulative Sampling Distribution for Two Flips of a Coin

or at least two heads. Figure 9-2 charts the sampling distribution in this way.

These sampling distributions are simple. The sampling distributions for most statistical tests are more complex, and we must use tables developed by statisticians to tell what the distributions look like. The cumulative sampling distribution of χ^2 for a three-by-three table (a table with three categories in the rows and three categories in the columns; for instance, Tables 9–2 and 9–3) is presented in Figure 9–3.

Chi-square sampling distributions vary, depending on the number of categories in the rows and columns of the table used. The probabilities given are the probability that a χ^2 *at least as* high as the one observed would have been obtained, if the sample were drawn from a parent population in which the variables were unrelated. (Note that this is a cumulative sampling distribution, like the distribution depicted in Figure 9–2.) Thus, if you had

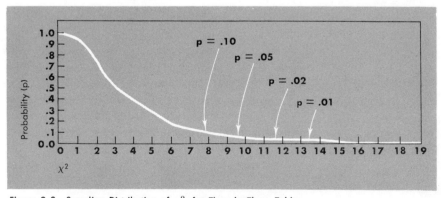

Figure 9–3   Sampling Distribution of χ^2, for Three-by-Three Tables

found a χ^2 of 4.9 you would know that the probability of getting χ^2 as high as this was .3, if the variables you were working with were, in fact, not related.

From this sampling distribution, we see that there is a probability of between .05 and .10 that we would have found a χ^2 of 8.44 from a three-by-three table, if there were really no relationship between ethnicity and choice of priority (that is, if the null hypothesis were true). This means that we would run a risk of between one chance in ten and one chance in twenty of being wrong in asserting on the basis of Table 9–2 that the null hypothesis is false, that there is a relationship between ethnicity and the choice of priorities.

To summarize these sections: A sampling distribution is simply a list of the probabilities that each possible event (out of a set of events) will happen. The probabilities in the sampling distribution are based on a set of assumptions. If we choose our significance test appropriately, the set of assumptions on which its sampling distribution is based will consist of: (1) a null hypothesis (the assumption that what we really want to say about the data is false), and (2) a group of other assumptions which we are certain are true. If we find from the sampling distribution that it is very unlikely, given those assumptions, that the event we have observed (in the example above, finding a χ^2 of 8.444) could have occurred, then we reject the assumptions on which the sampling distribution is based. Because we are sure that all but one of those assumptions (the null hypothesis) are true, this amounts to rejecting the null hypothesis and asserting its opposite, which is what we had originally wanted to say about the data. The probability that we could have gotten the observed result, if all of the assumptions underlying the sampling distribution were true, tells us how likely it is that we are wrong to reject the null hypothesis. Thus, a significance test furnishes a useful check on our research. It tells us how likely it is that we could have gotten our results by chance alone, the probability that in fact the opposite of what we are asserting is true.

THE IMPORTANCE OF N

The N, or number of cases in the sample, is always a factor in significance tests. All other things being equal, the greater the number of cases on which a statement is based, the more certain you can be that the statement is true.[4] Every significance test, accordingly, takes the number of cases into account. If each number in Tables 9–2 and 9–3 were doubled, for example, the quan-

[4] See the discussion of the Law of Large Numbers, p. 64.

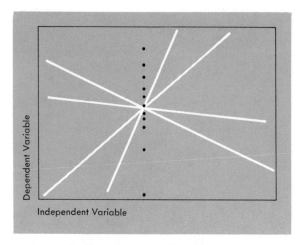

Figure 9–4   Regression Analysis with Zero Variance in the Independent Variable

tity ($F_o - F_h^2 / F_h$ would double for each cell. The χ^2 would be double 8.444, or 16.888. From Figure 9–3, we see that the probability of getting a χ^2 at least this high, if the null hypothesis of no relationship were true, is less than .01. Thus, from a table showing exactly the same pattern as Table 9–2, but based on a sample of four hundred cases instead of the two hundred used in that table, we would run a risk of less than one chance in a hundred of being wrong in asserting that there is a relationship between the variables.*

The N is the most obvious factor affecting the statistical significance of findings. In many sorts of statistical tests, it is the only factor we need to worry about. But there may be others.

For example, in regression analysis the amount of confidence we can have in our estimate of what the relationship looks like is a matter not only of how many cases we have used but also of how much the independent variable varies. In the extreme case of zero variance in the independent variable, depicted in the scattergram in Figure 9–4, we are simply unable to choose any regression line. Because all of the data points fall above a single value of the independent variable, an infinite number of lines (a few of which are indicated on the graph) can be passed through the data, each of which has an equal sum of squared deviations about itself. In other words, it is impossible to choose a single "best" line by least-squares criteria.

This is the extreme case. But in general, the greater variation there is

---

* The following seven paragraphs present advanced material which can be skipped over without any loss in comprehension of the remaining material covered in this book.

in the independent variable, the more firmly fixed the estimate of the regression line can be, and accordingly, the more stock we can put in our findings.

One way to look at this is to think of the regression line as wobbling on a fulcrum. As it happens, every regression line must pass through the point x, y in the scattergram; this is mathematically determined by the formulas for a and b. (In other words, the expected value of y when x equals its own mean *must* be the mean of y.) If there is relatively little variation in the independent variable, as in Figure 9–5, the line is free to wobble a good deal, using this point as a fulcrum. A considerable change in the angle at which the line passes through the point x, y will not change the size of residuals very much. This is due to the fact that for observations whose value on x is close to x̄, wobble in the line does not change the expected value of y very greatly; thus the difference between the observed and expected values of y also is not greatly changed.

No one of the observations is able to affect the regression line very much in Figure 9–5. The line simply is not held firmly in place by these observations, whose values on x fall so close together. Observations with widely varying values on x, however, would hold a much firmer grip on the regression line. Two such observations have been added in Figure 9–6.

If the regression line were now to wobble through the same angle as in Figure 9–5, the size of the deviations of observations A and B from the line would increase dramatically. Remember, the regression line must be the line which minimizes the sum of squared deviations about itself. The regression line in Figure 9–6 cannot stray very far from points A and B without sharply increasing that sum.

Thus, a few points whose x values are extreme have more impact in

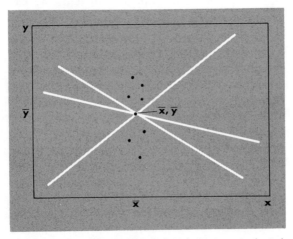

Figure 9–5   Regression Analysis with Little Variance in the Independent Variable

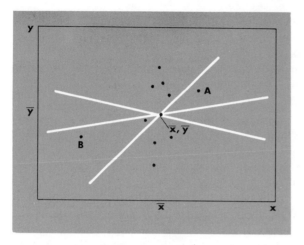

Figure 9–6   The Stabilizing Effect of Variance in the Independent Variable

determining the slope of the line than do a larger number of points whose x values fall close to the mean. Accordingly, in calculating how likely it is that our estimate of a regression has been due to chance, we must take into account not only how many observations have been used in the analysis, but also how widely they are spread on the independent variable. Significance tests designed for use with regression analysis take into account *both* the number of cases and the amount of varation in the independent variable.[5]

IS A SIGNIFICANCE TEST ALWAYS NECESSARY? Even when we do not work explicitly with a sample drawn from a larger group of subjects, there is a sense in which all research involves "sampling" of a sort, and in which misleading results can occur by chance. For instance, we might look at all fifty states and find that the generosity of their welfare budgets is related to the degree of party competition in the states' elections. In one sense, there is no question but that this is the "true" result. Because we have included in our sample all of the states, anything we find out about them is by definition "true generally." But suppose we think of ourselves as trying to say something not just about the fifty states as they exist at one point in time, but about "state politics." Then we must regard these fifty states as a sample drawn for us by chance and accident from a larger

---

[5] The general extension of this problem to multivariate regression is the problem of *collinearity,* which often has been overlooked in work with regression. For a good expository discussion of collinearity, see Forbes and Tufte, 1968.

metaphysical population of "states"—all states as they might be in the future, or as they might have been had their boundaries been drawn differently or had history proceeded differently.

The latter view seems to reflect more accurately what we try to do in developing political theories out of empirical research. There are times when one wishes to describe a specific population as it exists at one point in time; this is particularly likely in what I termed "engineering" research in Chapter 1. In such research, we frequently are interested in measuring some condition of a population so as to react to it or make adjustments in it, rather than to develop explanatory theories from it. For instance, it is sufficient for a tax administrator, for most purposes, to know how many states administer sales taxes, how great a portion of national income these states involve, and so on. What he is concerned with is a description of the tax situation as it currently exists. It is not his job (at least, in most of what he does) to develop theories to *explain* why things are as they are.[6] In most research which is oriented toward theory, however, we should seek a more inclusive sort of generality.

It is not rare to see an author claim that he does not need to be concerned about the possibility that his results are due to chance, because he has included a total population of subjects in his sample (all the states, all the nations in the United Nations, all the senators, or what have you). This is a statement that should arouse suspicion. If he is trying to draw general conclusions from his study, which one would expect to be as true of states or nations or senators a decade from now as it is today, then he *must* be concerned with the problem of chance results. With infrequent exceptions, then, this is a problem which we must take into account in our research.

USES AND LIMITATIONS OF STATISTICAL TESTS	I have tried in this chapter to present a significant test for what it is—a useful check on research results. The real meat of research, however—the way we find out about politics—is by looking at data and seeking out relationships between variables, the sorts of things I discussed in Chapters 5, 6, 7, and 8.

[6] Note, by the way; that to the extent that an engineer sees his task as *changing* and *reforming* patterns, rather than continuing ongoing administrative procedures, explanatory theory must be relatively more important for him. A tax administrator who wanted to change the extent to which states relied on sales taxes to generate their income would have to try to find out what makes states use sales taxes, so that he would know what changes to make. A *status quo* administrator can be more content with purely descriptive information, because his chief concern is with plugging established procedures into any given state of affairs, and what he needs is simply to know what the "state of affairs" is.

Unfortunately, researchers often lay undue emphasis on significance tests. It is a pity that looking at data requires less formal training (and more practice) than calculating significance tests does. Perhaps it is because they have spent so much time in courses learning to use significance tests, that many researchers give the tests an undue emphasis in their research. The status of these tests should be strictly that of a secondary check on the *creative* work the researcher has done in looking at relationships.

A recent article illustrates the problem. In this study, the author reported that two variables were more strongly related among the working-class portion of his sample than among the middle-class portion. His evidence for this was that among the working-class respondents, the relationship was more highly significant, with a probability of less than .01 that there was no relationship. Among the middle-class respondents, by contrast, the relationship was less highly significant, with probability between .01 and .05. Because previous theorists had said that one should expect a stronger relationship between the variables among the middle class than among the working class, this author was understandably excited about his findings.

Unfortunately, he was using his significance tests for something they were not meant to do. The significance test is not itself a measure of the strength of a relationship, but a check on how likely it is that a given measure is due to chance. In this example, as it happened, the middle-class portion of the author's sample was only about half as large as the working-class portion. It was because of the smaller number of cases in the middle-class portion that its relationship showed up as less significant than the relationship from among the working-class portion. In fact, when the strength of the relationship was measured by an appropriate technique (the Goodman-Kruskal Tau-A , for instance), it turned out that there was a *stronger* relationship among the middle class. The author's conclusion from his own data was wrong.

CONCLUSION

I have sketched out in this chapter the general logic of inference, which runs through all of the great variety of statistical tests. The tests vary among themselves, however, in terms of what level of measurement they are appropriate for and what particular mix of assumptions (other than the null hypothesis) they require the investigator to guarantee. This is why there are so many different ones. For a treatment of particular tests, the reader should consult one or more of the texts cited at the end of Chapter 7.

FURTHER DISCUSSION A particularly good discussion of the misapplication of significance tests, of the sort I mentioned above, is Duggan and Dean, "Common Misinterpretations of Significance Levels in Sociological Journals" (1968). See also Winch and Campbell, "Proof? No. Evidence? Yes. The Significance of Tests of Significance" (1969).

Anyone thinking of using the tests himself should have had a statistics course, but useful presentations of the techniques are given in all of the texts cited at the end of Chapter 7. The second chapter of Siegel (1956) is a particularly useful review of the overall logic of significance tests. It aims at much the same presentation as I have attempted in this chapter, but in rather more technical detail.

For further consideration, think about the two following situations. *What is wrong in each situation?*

1. A researcher studying Congress examines the vote on a hundred or so bills. For several of these votes, he finds that there was a statistically significant relationship (at the .05 level) between congressmen's height and the way they voted on the bill. This strikes him as a surprising finding, and he uses it for a chapter and a half of his book.

2. A large number of scholars study committee systems, in order to see whether democracy in committee decision making leads the members to be satisfied with their work on the committee. All but one of these scholars fail to find a statistically significant relationship between the democracy of committees' structure and the satisfaction of their members. Most of those who fail to find a relationship leave that question and start to work on other things. A few of them write up their results, but these are rejected by journal editors because they are negative, not positive, findings. The one scholar who did find a statistically significant result publishes it. Net result: one published article, reporting a statistically significant relationship between committee democracy and members' satisfaction.

WHERE DO THEORIES COME FROM? 10

This has been a book about developing theories and trying them out on reality. In Chapter 2, I portrayed the research process in general as a search for elegant theories. In succeeding chapters, I have discussed various aspects of research—concept formation, measurement, data analysis. My criterion throughout these chapters for the usefulness of any technique has been the extent to which that technique helped us build elegant theories. A high degree of "precision in measurement" is important, I have argued, because it allows us more flexibility in how we want to state the theory with which we are working. Measurement accuracy, whether it is a matter of reliability or validity, is important because, without accurate measurement, we cannot establish the connection between the data we are handling and the theory with which we are working. Regression analysis usually is more useful than correlation analysis, because the results of regression analysis apply generally to a theory, whereas the results of correlation analysis can serve only as a description of a particular situation. And so on.

In all of this, I have never dealt with a critical question: just how does one find a theory on which to work? There is one deceptively simple answer to this question, which is to choose theories for study out of the existing body of work in political science. That is, take a theory which was thought up by somebody else and try it out on some data. I discussed some of the limitations of this procedure in Chapter 2. But the important point for my discussion here is that this answer begs the question: "How did the original theorist find the theory?"

What makes a political scientist describe the relationship among a group of variables in a particular way? Probably it most frequently happens that the researcher observes a body of data and tries to see a pattern among them. This is the most obvious way to go about devising a theory; in fact, it follows quite naturally from the things a theory is supposed to achieve. The purpose of a theory is to provide a simplified pattern to describe a complicated jumble of observations. Would it not follow, then, that the most appropriate way to devise a theory is to look at the jumble of observations and try to find a simple pattern running through them?

Unfortunately, "observations" in political science are riddled with problems of accurate measurement; they are often measured imprecisely; and the nonexperimental circumstances under which we gather them make it difficult to isolate the effects of single variables. These are all problems that I have discussed earlier in this book. Their combined effect is to make it very difficult to look at a batch of observations and pick out the best simplifying pattern. There is just so much going on in a group of observations, much of which is extraneous to what we want to do, that the pattern we ideally would hope to pick out is obscured.

This problem is not confined to the social sciences. James S. Coleman describes the way the theory of gravity might *not* have been devised, had Galileo gone about his task in the way most data-analyzing social scientists do:

> A simple example will illustrate some of the difficulties which might arise by this kind of "brick-by-brick" approach to theory. Suppose that early mechanics had developed by the use of regression equations. Suppose, specifically, that an investigation had been carried out relating the length of time a body had fallen through air and the velocity it attained. The relation in mechanics is that the velocity attained is equal to the acceleration due to gravity times the time the object has fallen, or
>
> $$v = gt \tag{3.4}$$
>
> where g is the acceleration due to gravity. Now if there had been numerous investigations involving different-sized bodies, different velocities, and bodies with differing densities, the investigators would have ended with numerous pairs of observations (v_i, t_i), which they would locate on a scatter diagram in order to find the line of best fit. But in every case, and especially for high velocities (i.e., objects which fell a great distance) and low-density objects (i.e., feathers), the observed velocity would fall considerably below that which the theoretical equation (3.4) predicts. The resulting regression equation might have ended up including other variables, such as mass or density of the object; and there would have been indications that at high velocities the relation of velocity to time was not even linear. The reason, of course, would be air resistance, which has different effects as a function of the density of the object, its shape, its velocity, and other things. The regression equation would of course have been empirically correct, but it wouldn't have corresponded to the simple velocity-time relation which served as the basis for Galileo's remarkable contribution to the science of

mechanics. They might even have served to confound the issue, by bringing in too soon a factor—i.e., air resistance—which was irrelevant to the fundamentals of mechanics.[1]

The moral of the story is that we almost always are better off if we have some idea of what kind of pattern we want to look for before we ever start to look at data. If we have in mind a particular kind of pattern, then it is easy to tell, of the jumble of things we find, what is relevant to the pattern and what is extraneous. Galileo was able to ignore the effects of air resistance because he knew that they were not the thing he should use to explain the speed of falling objects.

The distinction here is between "inductive" and "deductive" theory building. To build theory inductively, the researcher scans his observations, looking for patterns. To build theory deductively, he deduces (from something else, some prior expectations) what sort of a pattern he should expect and then looks for it in his observations.

According to the argument I have presented so far in this chapter, deductive theory building is clearly the better of the two. The problem lies with that "something else" from which you are supposed to deduce theories. There simply are not many well-established *premises* in the social sciences from which to deduce anything. One way of distinguishing an ongoing "science" from a "pre-science" is that the former includes a generally agreed-upon body of assumptions from which most of its theories can be deduced.[2] Political science, sociology, and similar social sciences certainly cannot be said to possess such a body of assumptions.

Lacking this base for deduction, it is hard to argue patly that theory building must be done deductively, "because that is the scientific way to do it." On the other hand, it is important to bear in mind the advantages of deduction, where it is feasible.

There are some tricks which can help you be alert for situations in which deduction is feasible. One of the best sources of deductive theory is a well-established theory from another field. Converse, for example, drew upon psychological theory for his theory "Of Time and Partisan Stability," which I described as an example in Chapter 2. Theories of epidemic growth and population dynamics, from such fields as epidemiology and ecology, may suggest theories to political scientists or sociologists. So may cybernetic theory. A healthy awareness of major theories in fields such as these, some of which are not all that closely related to our field, can be a helpful source of theories.

[1] James S. Coleman, *Introduction to Mathematical Sociology* (New York: The Free Press, 1964), pp. 100–101. Copyright 1964 by The Free Press.
[2] For an elaboration of this theme, see Kuhn, 1962.

The art of building a theory remains in flux in political science—partly deductive, but largely inductive. In many ways, the resulting confusion can be both enjoyable and fruitful because, more than in most disciplines, it allows a place for every sort of imagination to work: literary imagination, scientific imagination, moral imagination, mathematical imagination. It is in this spirit that I have tried to stress the "craft" in the "craft of political research."

SELECTED BIBLIOGRAPHY

AGGER, ROBERT E., MIROSLAV DISMAN, ZDRAVKO MLINAR, and VLADIMIR SULTANOVIC. 1970. "Education, General Personal Orientations, and Community Involvement," *Comparative Political Studies*, III (April), 90–116.

BARBER, JAMES D. 1972. *The Presidential Character: Predicting Performance in the White House*. Englewood Cliffs, N. J.: Prentice-Hall, Inc.

BARTON, ALLAN H. 1955. "The Concept of Property-Space in Social Research." In Paul F. Lazarsfeld and Morris Rosenberg, eds., *The Language of Social Research*. New York: The Free Press, pp. 40–53.

BLALOCK, HUBERT M. 1960. *Social Statistics*. New York: McGraw-Hill Book Company.

———. 1964. *Causal Inferences in Nonexperimental Research*. Chapel Hill: University of North Carolina Press.

———. 1969. *Theory Construction: From Verbal to Mathematical Formulations*. Englewood Cliffs, N.J.: Prentice-Hall, Inc.

BUTLER, DAVID, and DONALD STOKES. 1969. *Political Change in Britain*. New York: St. Martin's Press.

CAMPBELL, ANGUS, *et al.* 1960. *The American Voter*. New York: John Wiley & Sons, Inc.

CAMPBELL, DONALD T., and JULIAN C. STANLEY. 1963. *Experimental and Quasi-Experimental Designs for Research*. Chicago: Rand McNally & Co.

COLEMAN, JAMES S. 1964. *Introduction to Mathematical Sociology*. New York: The Free Press.

CONVERSE, PHILIP E. 1964. "The Nature of Belief Systems in Mass Publics." In David Apter, ed., *Ideology and Discontent*. New York: The Free Press, pp. 206–61.

———. 1969. "Of Time and Partisan Stability," *Comparative Political Studies*, II, 139–71.

———, and GEORGES DUPEUX. 1962. "Politicization of the Electorate in France and the United States," *Public Opinion Quarterly*, XXVI (Spring), 1–23.

DAHL, ROBERT. 1966. *Political Oppositions in Western Democracies*. New Haven: Yale University Press.

———. 1970. *Modern Political Analysis*. 2nd ed. Englewood Cliffs, N.J.: Prentice-Hall, Inc.

DOWNS, ANTHONY. 1957. *An Economic Theory of Democracy.* New York: Harper & Row, Publishers, Inc.

DUGGAN, THOMAS J., and CHARLES W. DEAN. 1968. "Common Misinterpretations of Significance Levels in Sociological Journals," *American Sociologist,* III (February), 45–46.

DUVERGER, MAURICE. 1963. *Political Parties.* New York: Science Editions.

ECKSTEIN, HARRY. 1960. *Pressure Group Politics.* London: George Allen & Unwin.

———. 1966. *Division and Cohesion in Democracy.* Princeton: Princeton University Press.

EDWARDS, ALLEN L. 1967. *Statistical Methods.* New York: Holt, Rinehart & Winston, Inc.

ELDERSVELD, SAMUEL. 1964. *Political Parties: A Behavioral Analysis.* Chicago: Rand McNally & Co.

FORBES, HUGH DONALD, and EDWARD R. TUFTE. 1968. "A Note of Caution in Causal Modelling," *American Political Science Review,* LXII (December), 1262–63.

FRY, BRIAN R., and RICHARD F. WINTERS. 1970. "The Politics of Redistribution," *American Political Science Review;* LIV (June), 508–23.

GOODMAN, LEO A., and WILLIAM H. KRUSKAL. 1954. "Measures of Association for Cross Classifications," *Journal of the American Statistical Association,* XLIX (December), 747–54.

HAYS, WILLIAM L. 1963. *Statistics.* New York: Holt, Rinehart & Winston, Inc.

JACOB, PHILIP E. 1955. "A Multi-Dimensional Classification of Atrocity Stories." In Paul F. Lazarsfeld and Morris Rosenberg, eds., *The Language of Social Research.* New York: The Free Press, pp. 54–57.

JAROS, DEAN, HERBERT HIRSCH, and FREDERICK J. FLERON, JR. 1968. "The Malevolent Leader: Political Socialization in an American Subculture," *American Political Science Review,* LXII (June), 564–75.

KARSTEN, PETER, et al. 1971. "ROTC, Mylai and the Volunteer Army," *Foreign Policy,* No. 2 (Spring), pp. 135–61.

KEY, V. O., JR. 1950. *Southern Politics.* New York: Alfred A. Knopf.

———. 1955. "A Theory of Critical Elections," *Journal of Politics,* XVII, 3–18

———. 1959. "Secular Realignment and the Party System," *Journal of Politics,* XXI, 198–210.

KOENIG, LOUIS W. 1968. *The Chief Executive.* Rev. ed. New York: Harcourt Brace Jovanovich.

KROEBER, A. L., and CLYDE KLUCKHOHN. 1952. *Culture: A Critical Review of C(ʿpts and Definitions.* Cambridge, Mass.: The Museum.

KUHN, THOMAS S. 1962. *The Structure of Scientific Revolutions.* Chicago: The University of Chicago Press.

LANE, ROBERT E. 1965. "The Politics of Consensus in an Age of Affluence," *American Political Science Review,* LIX (December), 874–95.

MATTHEWS, DONALD R., and JAMES W. PROTHRO. 1963. "Social and Economic Factors and Voter Registration in the South," *American Political Science Review,* LVII (March), 24ff.

MORGENSTERN, OSKAR. 1950. *On the Accuracy of Economic Observations.* Princeton: Princeton University Press.

MOSTELLER, FREDERICK. 1968. s.v. "Errors," *International Encyclopedia of the Social Sciences.* New York: The Macmillan Company.

NEUSTADT, RICHARD E. 1965. *Presidential Power.* New York: John Wiley & Sons, Inc.

NORDLINGER, ERIC A. 1970. "Soldiers in Mufti: The Impact of Military Rule upon Economic and Social Change in the Non-Western States," *American Political Science Review,* LXIV, 1131–49.

POMPER, GERALD. 1967. "Classification of Presidential Elections," *Journal of Politics,* XXIX, 535–67.

PROTHRO, JAMES W. 1956. "The Nonsense Fight over Scientific Method: A Plea for Peace," *Journal of Politics,* XVIII, 565–70.

ROBINSON, W. S. 1950. "Ecological Correlations and the Behavior of Individuals," *American Sociological Review,* XV (June), 351–57.

ROETHLISBERGER, F. J., and W. J. DICKSON. 1939. *Management and the Worker.* Cambridge: Harvard University Press.

SIEGEL, SIDNEY. 1956. *Nonparametric Statistics for the Behavioral Sciences.* New York: McGraw-Hill Book Company.

STOKES, DONALD E. 1969. "Cross-Level Inference as a Game Against Nature." In Joseph L. Bernd, ed., *Mathematical Applications in Political Science.* Charlottesville, Va.: The University of Virginia Press, IV, 62–83.

STOUFFER, SAMUEL, *et al.* 1949. *The American Soldier.* Princeton: Princeton University Press.

TARROW, SIDNEY. 1971. "The Urban-Rural Cleavage in Political Involvement: The Case of France," *American Political Science Review,* LXV (June), 341–57.

TINBERGEN, NIKO. 1968. *Curious Naturalists.* Garden City, N.Y.: Doubleday & Company, Inc.

TINGSTEN, HERBERT. 1937. *Political Behavior.* London: Longmans.

TUFTE, EDWARD R. 1968–69. "Improving Data Analysis in Political Science," *World Politics,* XXI, 641–54.

WATSON, JAMES D. 1968. *The Double Helix.* New York: Atheneum.

WEBB, EUGENE J., DONALD T. CAMPBELL, RICHARD D. SCHWARTZ, and LEE SECHRIST. 1966. *Unobtrusive Measures.* Chicago: Rand McNally & Co.

WINCH, ROBERT F., and DONALD T. CAMPBELL. 1969. "Proof? No. Evidence? Yes: The Significance of Tests of Significance," *American Sociologist,* IV (May), 140–43.

INDEX

Age and voting turnout, 63-64
Agger, Robert, 94
Anomalies, 27

Barber, James D., 27n
Barton, Allan H., 44
Binary variables, 137
Blalock, Hubert, 101, 119n, 120n, 124, 142n
Butler, David, 41n

Campbell, Angus, 39n
Campbell, Donald T., 59, 91n, 92n, 101, 162
Causation, 14, 80-85
Chi-square, 148, 150-53
Coleman, James S., 165-66
Collinearity, 159
Concepts and measures, 48-49
Control groups, 86-89
Controlling for a variable, 98-102
Converse, Philip, 17-20, 35n, 142, 166
Converting election, 39
Correlation coefficient, 115-23
"Correlational" measurement of a relationship, 105
Critical election, 38, 40
Cumulative sampling distribution, 154-55

Dahl, Robert, 44
Dean, Charles W., 162
Deductive theory construction, 166
Dependent variable, 14
Deviating election, 39
Dichotomous variables, 135-37
Dickson, W. J., 87n
Direct measurement, 49-50
Downs, Anthony, 7-8

Duggan, Thomas J., 162
Dummy variables, 137
Dupeux, Georges, 17
Duverger, Maurice, 3-5

Eckstein, Harry, 44, 61
Ecological fallacy, 122
Education and voting turnout, 136
Edwards, Allen L., 124
"Effect-descriptive" measure of relationships, 105
Eldersveld, Samuel, 91
Elections, types of, 38-43
Elegant theories, 16
Engineering research, 6-7
Experiments, 90-91
Ex post facto argument, 24

Fleron, Frederick J., Jr., 28n
Forbes, Hugh Donald, 159n
"Formal" theory, 6
Fry, Brian, 91

Gamma, Goodman-Kruskal, 128-30
Goodman, Leo A., 128, 131, 133n

Hawthorne study, 87n
Hays, William L., 124
Hirsch, Herbert, 28n
Holding constant a variable, 98-102

Independent variable, 14
Inductive theory construction, 166
Inference, statistical, 104
Integration, national, 37
Interaction, 142
Intercept of a regression equation, 109

International Encyclopedia of the Social Sciences, 59
Interval measurement, 66-67

Jacob, Philip E., 44
Jaros, Dean, 28n

Karsten, Peter, 73
Key, V. O., Jr, 38, 39, 113-15
Kluckhohn, Clyde, 38
Koenig, Louis W., 27n
Kroeber, A. L., 38
Kruskal, William H., 128, 131, 133n
Kuhn, Thomas S., 166n

Lane, Robert E., 96-97
Law of Large Numbers, 64
Linear relationships, 73, 74
Literary Digest poll, 55

Maintaining election, 39
Markov chains, 19
Marx, Karl, 9
Matthews, Donald, 141n
Mean, arithmetic, 118
Mill, John Stuart, 6
Morgenstern, Oskar, 59
Mosteller, Frederick, 59
Multivariate regression analysis, 137-42

Natural experiment, 88-90
Neustadt, Richard, 27
Nominal data, measures of relationship for, 130-35
Nominal measurement, 66
Nordlinger, Eric, 8-9
Null hypothesis, 149-50

Ordinal data, measures of relationship for, 126-30
Ordinal measurement, 66

Panel studies, 98
Party identification, 17
Philosophy, normative, 6
Pomper, Gerald, 39
Precision in measurement, 66-78
in measures, 63-66, 76-78
Product-moment correlation coefficient, 115-23
Prothro, James, 20, 141n

"Quantitative" research, 20-22, 76-77

ROTC and military orientation, 73
Ratio measurement, 67n, 77-78
Realigning election, 39
Regression analysis, 108-15
Relative deprivation, 10
Reliability, 50-54, 58-59
as a characteristic of a concept, 52
tests for, 52-54
Research design, 85-98
Residuals, analysis of, 112-15
Robinson, W. S., 122n
Roethlisberger, F. J., 87n

Sampling distribution, 153-56
Schwartz, Richard D., 59
Sechrist, Lee, 59
Secular realignment, 38, 40
Siegel, Sidney, 133n, 162
Significance test, 146ff
Slope of a regression equation, 109
Social status, 46-47
Split-half check for reliability, 53
Stanley, Julius C., 91n, 92n, 101
Statistics, defined, 104
Stokes, Donald, 41n, 122n
Stouffer, Samuel, 9-10
Stratified sampling, 65

Tarrow, Sidney, 27, 56
Tau-A, Goodman-Kruskal, 131-35
Test-retest check for reliability, 52-53
Theories, 3-5
criteria for good, 11, 15-16
Theory-oriented research, 6
Tinbergen, Niko, 101
Tingsten, Herbert, 101
Topic, choice of, 22-23
Tufte, Edward R., 77, 159n

Unidimensionality, 31
Units and regression analysis, 110

Validity, 54-59
Variables, 14
Variance, 118-20
Voting turnout
and age, 63-64
and education, 136

Watson, James D., 1
Webb, Eugene J., 59
Winch, Robert F., 162
Winters, Richard, F., 91